It's <u>Your</u> Future -
The Workbook!

Charles G. Bird, MBA

This book uses O*NET-TM Career Exploration Tools, version as of August 2015. The trademark logo or icon for the

O*NET-TM IN IT bug is:

The U.S. Department of Labor, Employment and Training Administration is the exclusive owner of all rights under U.S. copyright laws and international treaty provisions in the O*NET-TM Career Exploration Tools. Any other copyright notices refer only to Charles Bird's original work in the product.

O*NET and O*NET IN IT and their associated logos are trademarks of the U.S. Department of Labor, Employment and Training Administration.

This book may include material used by:
O*NET Interest ProfilerTM
O*NET Work Importance LocatorTM
O*NET Computerized Interest ProfilerTM
O*NET Work Importance ProfilerTM (computerized)
O*NET Ability ProfilerTM.

It's Your Future, Copyright © 2015 by Charles G Bird. All rights reserved.
ISBN-10: 1517207592
ISBN-13: 978-1517207595

About the Author: Charles G. Bird, MBA

I earned a BA in Psychology and and MBA at Wayne State University in Detroit, Michigan. I completed training at the University of Wisconsin-Stout in Vocational Evaluation and Work Adjustment. I also studied Guidance & Counseling at Oakland University.

I am a past member of the American Personnel & Guidance Association, and the Vocational Evaluation & Work Adjustment Association.

My work experiences include: Vocational Evaluator, Rehabilitation Counselor, and careers as a State Energy Project Coordinator, Material Handling Business Manager, and Information Systems Manager. He has worked in the private sector, the public sector, been self-employed and had business partners.

I recently co-designed and delivered a series of 8 workshops specifically designed for short-term and long-term unemployed, including the never employed, and those seeking their first jobs. Topics covered included Coping & Dealing with Long Term Unemployment, Motivation, Job Loss Grief, Using O*NET, Using My Next Move, Networking for Beginners, Job Keeping Skills, "What Do Employers Want?", Informational Interviewing, Problem Solving, Goal Attainment, "Finding Your Most Rewarding Job", and more.

I have completed this book companion to "It's Your Life". I am producing a documentary about the Great Storm of 1913 and any such other projects as catch my interest.

This book is dedicated to my wife, Linda.

I hope that you find the material interesting, motivating, and useful to you in getting your most rewarding jobs and careers.

Table of Contents

Documentation Exercises 5

Where Are You? 7

Name Them: 15

Why I Work 16

Why I Volunteer or Would 19

Skills: 21

Knowledge 24

Tools & Technology 29

Abilities 63

Work Activities 68

Problem Solving...86

Goals 96

Job and Career Goal Attainment 98

Organized Plan 100

Informational Interviewing: 102

Job Target Worksheet: 109

Job History Worksheet..112

Resumes: 114

Sample Job Application Form 116

Telephone Contact Summary 118

Telephone Call Log...119

Interview Checklist 120

Job Questions You Should Ask 121

Interview Questions you will be asked 125

My Marketing Plan 129

Stress...136

Documentation Exercises

Why start here? Good documentation takes practice. We suggest that as you do some, or all, of the exercises in this workbook, why not make entries in your documentation?

After you've done a few exercise and made a few entries, see if you can go back and understand what you did when. This is the essence of documentation, in other words, "who did what when". Other things you may consider adding are other important facts like; where did it occur, how much money was involved, how did it happen and why did it happen. The basic element though is to answer the question of "who did what when?".

One other thing to mention is that it is worth knowing how long things take. It can help you in your future planning. When you review your documentation, you can realistically decide if you need to put more time in. You will see how you are investing your time and make adjustments to some of what you are doing. When you show documentation like this to a Job Professional or Career Development Facilitator they can give you better feedback if they know what you've been doing, concentrating on, and where adjustments might be useful.

Here is a short practice documentation table. Enter todays date, the time you turned to this exercise, the time you finished, and what you did. Two examples are given, now you try documenting the next five things you do, even if they aren't about jobs, you're practicing "documenting", so if you stopped and made a cake, make an entry.

There is a complete table on the next page that you can make copies of and keep your job and career oriented work documented. You can also use the worksheet as a model and set up a table in a word processing program or even a spreadsheet program.

Date	Start	End	What I did
9/30/14	9:03 am	9:04 am	Made my first documentation entry!!
9/30/14	9:04 am	9:40 am	Completed one Job History form, for my last job.
Date	Start	End	What I did

Date	Start	End	What I did

Where Are You?

Where are you in life? Where are you in the job hunt? Where are you in your career? These are three key questions for you to consider before you continue looking for a job. Each has a bearing on your work options, so take a moment and take a look at yourself.

What are you looking for? A job? A career? A job leading to a career? (Ex. 1: I am looking for a entry-level job in the career field of biometrics. Ex. 2: I am looking for a job in a restaurant. Ex. 3: I am looking for a career in healthcare.) Your turn, what are you looking for? Be as specific as you can. _____

_____

_____

Where exactly are you in the hunt for your next job or your career? Are you currently working or unemployed? (Ex. 1: I am unemployed and have never worked and I just started looking. Ex. 2: I am under-employed, working part time until I find a full time job as realtor and I've been looking for six months. Ex. 3: I am unemployed, looking for an entry level job in a new industry, I've been looking for over a year.) Your turn: _____

_____

_____

_____

What is your age? _____

Work Experience:

_____ Never had a job.
_____ Raised a family but never had a job.
_____ Retired, had one career.
_____ Retired, had one job.
_____ Retired, more than one career.
_____ Retired, more than one job.
_____ I've had 1-3 jobs in the same industry.
_____ I've had 1-3 jobs in different industries. How many industries? _____
_____ I've had 4-7 jobs in the same industry.
_____ I've had 4-7 jobs in different industries. How many industries? _____
_____ I've had 8-12 jobs in the same industry.
_____ I've had 8-12 jobs in different industries. How many industries? _____
_____ I've had more than 12 jobs in the same industry.
_____ I've had more than 12 jobs in different industries. How many industries? _____

How do you explain your work history? _____

_____

_____

_____

Education:

What education do you have? Include any kind of training programs you may have be in. If there were particular classes or courses you enjoyed and or did particularly well in, list them and note if you like d it or did well in it.

_____ Less than High School Graduate
_____ High School Graduate
_____ Less than two years of college
_____ Associates Degree (Completed two-year college program)
_____ More than two years but less than four years of college.
_____ Bachelors Degree (Completed 4 or 5 year college program, with diploma)
_____ Education beyond Bachelors but no additional degree.
_____ Master's Degree
_____ Doctorate.

Training (list every training program you have completed and when completed, whether it was a one-day or multi-year training program)

What Training	When
Ex: completed four year electrical apprenticeship	1995
Ex: completed two day training program on MS SQL Online Analytical Processing (OLAP)	2007

What skills do you possess? (If you are not sure, turn to the "Skills" chapter) _____
_____
_____
_____
_____
_____

What "work knowledge" do you have? (If you are not sure, turn to the "Knowledge chapter).
_____
_____
_____
_____
_____

What "work abilities" do you have? (If you are not sure, turn to the "Abilities" chapter.)
_____
_____
_____
_____
_____

What kind of worker are you? What are your values? (Not sure, turn to the chapters on "Why I work" and "Why I volunteer). _____
_____
_____
_____
_____
_____

What work activities interest you? (Not sure, turn to the chapter on "Work Activities").
_____
_____
_____
_____
_____

Do you want or need to change fields? Yes No

Do you know what your next job could or should be? Yes No

Do you know what kinds of jobs you could get being exactly who you are now? Yes No

Do you know what kinds of jobs you could get with a little training, or education or experience? Yes No

If you could not answer the last four questions with "Yes", you need help. Use this workbook and the "It's Your Future" textbook to find some of the help you need. Consider using the Dept. of Labor O*NET resources, (onetonline.org) and My Next Move (mynextmove.org) and Career

One Stop (http://www.careeronestop.org/). Do not hesitate to visit one of the Workforce Investment Act centers in your area for their assistance too (http://www.servicelocator.org/).

Where do you live:

_____ within 5 miles of a metropolitan area (population over 1,000,000 in the area)
_____ 5 - 10 miles of a metropolitan area (population over 1,000,000 in the area)
_____ 10 - 25 miles of a metropolitan area (population over 1,000,000 in the area)
_____ within 5 miles of a smaller urban area (population between 100,000 and 500,000)
_____ 5 - 10 miles of a smaller urban area (population between 100,000 and 500,000)
_____ 10 - 25 miles of a smaller urban area (population between 100,000 and 500,000)
_____ a rural area.

It should go without saying but we'll say it anyway, there are more jobs in large metropolitan areas than smaller ones or rural areas. However, there are more agricultural jobs in rural areas. There is more competition for jobs in areas with larger populations.

How far are you willing to commute to work one way?

_____ Less than 5 miles
_____ 5 - 10 miles
_____ 11 - 25 miles
_____ 25 - 50 miles
_____ More than 50 miles

The further you are willing to travel, the more opportunities you have available. The less you are willing to travel, the more you need to consider re-locating to get a favorable job.

Are you willing to relocate for the right job? Yes No Maybe.

How long have you been looking for work?

_____ Less than 1 week
_____ 1 - 4 weeks
_____ 5 - 13 weeks
_____ 13-26 weeks
_____ more than six months, less than one year.
_____ more than one year.

If you have been looking more than six months for a job you ask yourself the following questions:
• Do I have the right job goal?
• Do I need alternative job goals?
• Am I going about job hunting the right way?
• Am I getting interviews?
• Am I looking in the right area?
• Is there anything wrong with my resume?
• How many jobs have I applied for?
• How many resumes have I sent out with cover letters?

- How many resumes did I hand carry to potential employers?
- How many applications have I completed online?
- How many applications have I completed in person?
- Did I send a thank you letter after each interview?
- How many jobs have I turned down?

My Job Targets (the jobs I'm trying to get) and three alternative job titles or similar jobs.

Job	Job Goals/Targets	Alternatives
1		
2		
3		

Given you are seeking 1 - 3 jobs that you want, and know your qualified for, what are similar jobs that with a little training or time on the job that you might be qualified for? You want to build up the number of alternatives you have to increase your chance of getting one. More options equals more chance.

Here's an example:

Job	Job Goals/Targets	Alternatives
1	Bicycle Mechanic	Bicycle Service Technician
		Bike Mechanic
		Bicycle Repairman
2	Bicycle Mechanic	Motorcycle Mechanic
		Small Engine Mechanic
		RV Service Technician
3	Bicycle Mechanic	Mechanical Door Repairer

Job	Job Goals/Targets	Alternatives
		Home Appliance Repairer
		Locksmith

Some of those may not be jobs you can get now, but you could with some training.

For each of the jobs you are seeking, how many can you identify within your one-way commute range?

Here's an example for the above job, Bicycle Mechanic, and it's alternatives:

Job	Employer/Company	Applied in Person
1	Ajax Bicycle Shop	Y/N
1	Melvin's Custom Made Bikes	Y/N
1	All-Brands Appliance Repair	Y/N
1	OpenIt Locksmiths	Y/N

We listed lines for 4 employers in the previous table but there could be hundreds, especially if you expand you own thinking by investigating where the job you are seeking can be found. For example if you are looking for a job as a nurse, are you looking only at hospitals? Why not nursing home, schools, or visiting nurse associations, colleges, hospices, the military, state government opportunities. Or if you are looking for work driving a forklift truck, you are certain to look at warehouses and distributors but how about factories, or airports? Again, you are looking for more options.

You should create a table for each type of job you are seeking. Another way for you to do this is to get out a sheet of paper or fire up a word processing or spreadsheet program and make a list of every employer that hires people to do the work, the job, you are seeking. Depending on where you live and how far you are willing to travel, how many job options you are giving yourself, you could have hundreds if not thousands of possibilities.

Family situation:
_____ live at home with parent(s) or other relative(s).
_____ live alone or with roommates (no obligations to stay with them).
_____ live with working spouse, no children or other dependents.
_____ live with non-working spouse, no children or other dependents.
_____ live with working spouse and dependents in home.
_____ live with non-working spouse and dependents in home.

How flexible you are in the type of job you can accept, whether you can re-locate or not, and whether benefits could be negatively impacted by a move, are all factors you need to take into account.

Now that you have given thought to who you are, write up and summary of all the information you've gathered here:

My name is _____. The following describes "where I am" or what my Most Rewarding Job would look like:

_____
_____
_____
_____
_____
_____
_____
_____
_____
_____
_____
_____
_____
_____
_____
_____
_____
_____
_____
_____
_____
_____
_____

On the next page is a one-page blank Job Target Table for you to use!

Job Target: _____

Job	Employer/Company	Applied in Person
		Y/N
		Y/N
		Y/N
		Y/N
		Y/N
		Y/N
		Y/N
		Y/N
		Y/N
		Y/N
		Y/N
		Y/N
		Y/N
		Y/N
		Y/N
		Y/N
		Y/N
		Y/N
		Y/N
		Y/N
		Y/N
		Y/N

Name Them:

Name the job(s) that you know your education, skills and knowledge match.

In the book, you were asked how many jobs call for your skills, knowledge and education and to name them. In other sections of this workbook we spend time on your abilities, tools, technology, work activities and values. You've been shown how to use various resources to take that information and develop more job options. In fact, you'll probably have so many options, you'll run out of room! When you do, use a word processor, a spreadsheet program or a plain old sheet of paper to keep a record.

Here's your challenge. In the first column enter the date you make an entry in the second column (use todays date if you write one or more of your job options down today). But by all means, keep the records as it is visual evidence of your growth in self-knowledge and your career options.You are on a path of self-discovery and as you learn more about yourself, and work, come back to this exercise and add more to it.

Date	Job Options

Why I Work

In this exercise, circle, check or highlight any and all statements that seem to you to be reasons you work or things you like about work. Then go back and rank them in order of importance to you. You can give the same rank to more than one. For example, if you think being around others and using your skills are both the most important thing to you, give them both a "1". Only rank the reasons that are important to you.

We include extra rows for you to use in case we've missed something that is important to you. Go ahead and write them in.

My Reasons	Check	Rank
I feel valuable		
I feel connected		
It's all about the money		
I like to be around others		
I like to use my skills		
I like to accomplish things		
It gives meaning to my life		
I like to be creative		
I get bored with nothing to do		
I identify with where I work		
It gives me purpose, a reason to live		
I like to learn new things.		
I like to know everything I need to know to do my job		
Benefits are really important to me, especially insurance		
Who I work for, my boss, is very important to me		
Benefits are really important to me, especially a pension or retirement plan.		
I like to work where I can learn new things.		
Where I work is important to me.		

My Reasons	Check	Rank
I prefer to work alone		
I like a challenging job.		
I like to help people.		
I like to be recognized for my accomplishments and achievements		
It's what I live for.		
I work for money.		
I prefer to work with others as part of a team		
Accomplishments		
The company values are important to me		
I like to work and be productive.		
How the company treats its employees is important to me		
I work to live.		
What I do for a living is important to me.		
I prefer to work with others but not as part of a team		
Work is fulfilling		
My job duties are really important to what I do.		
Most of my friends are people I meet at or through work.		
I need to feel pride in what I do.		
I live to work.		
I like to win awards		
Working gives me confidence.		
Working conditions are important to me		
I like to meet new people.		
This is what I do, my reason for existing and being.		
Where I work is more important that what I do		

My Reasons	Check	Rank
I'm very competitive		
My work gives meaning to my life.		
I like to work with a variety of people from different backgrounds.		
Achievements.		
What I do isn't all that important to me, as long as I'm earning enough.		
I like helping people.		
I can't stand not being productive and doing things.		
I want the opportunity to advance.		
I work for the things I can buy for me or my family.		
Self-expression.		
I want people to look up to me for the work I do.		
I like to solve problems.		
I like to work with my hands.		

Why I Volunteer or Would

Simply circle or check the reasons you volunteer or would volunteer. As always, we include extra rows for you to use in case we've missed something that is important to you. Go ahead and write them in.

Reason	Check
I wanted to improve things or help people	
The cause was really important to me	
I had spare time to do it	
I wanted to meet people or make friends	
I thought it would give me a chance to use my existing skills	
I felt there was a need in my community	
It was connected with the needs of my family or friends	
It's part of my philosophy of life to help people	
I thought it would give me a chance to learn new skills	
My friends or family did it	
It's part of my religious belief to help people	
I felt there was no one else to do it	
It helps me get on in my career	
I had received voluntary help	
It gave me the chance to get recognized in a qualification	

My Most Rewarding Work

You just completed two exercises that can help you understand more about yourself and why you work.

Go back over both the "Why I Work" and "Why I Volunteer" exercises and write down all the reasons you selected as important to you. Try to put them in order of importance to you. There is no right or wrong answers to this. Your reasons for working are yours, they are personal, no better or worse than anyone else's reasons.

Why I work: _____

_____

_____

_____

_____

_____

_____

_____

_____

_____

_____

_____

_____

_____

_____

_____

_____

_____

_____

_____

_____

_____

_____

_____

_____

_____

_____

_____

Take a careful look at those first few sentences, as they should be the most important factors for you and help guide you in deciding what kind of work you should look for. If you accept a job that does not include most, if not all, of the factors you've written down, you are less likely to be satisfied with that job. If that is the case, you should consider career and job alternatives. Who wouldn't want a job that was the most rewarding to them? You do want your most rewarding job and career don't you?

Skills:

- Personal SKILLS Inventory -

If you think of "skills" as "ability", you are on the right track. A skill is an ability to do something or do it rapidly.

The following is a comprehensive list of the skills as listed and categorized by the US Department of Labor and O*NET as of 2014. O*NET OnLine is sponsored by the U.S. Department of Labor, Employment & Training Administration, and developed by the National Center for O*NET Development.

Circle or highlight the skills you believe you have to some degree. Don't sell yourself short, or discount yourself. Some jobs will only require you to have an entry-level amount of the skill, others just "some" while still others require lots of the skill. O*NET can help you sort out your skill level as they relate to work, job and careers.

After you have marked the skills you have, first stop and be impressed with how much skill you already possess. Then mark the ones you like using with an "**L**" in the second column, or an "**N**" for "**N**ot-so-much do I like using this skill".

Then go back and rate your skill in the area as "S" (Strong), "A" (Average), or "W" (Weak). Again, this is your opinion, just try to be honest with yourself but try to underrate yourself either.

Use the fourth column to decide if you want to "Target" (YES or No) using those skills to find job and career alternatives.

Finally, use O*NET and your Personal Skill Inventory to find jobs and careers that match the skills you have, most like using, and are strongest.

You should also write out on a separate sheet of paper, or go back to the "Name Them" exercise, and write in your "best" skills. How many of them did you identify already and how many were skills you hadn't even thought about as "job" skills?

Circle or Highlight Your Skill	Like/Don't Like	S-A-W	Target? Y/N
Basic Skills — Those that facilitate learning or the more rapid acquisition of knowledge			
Content Types of Basic Skills:			
Reading			
Comprehension			
Active Listening			

Circle or Highlight Your Skill	Like/Don't Like	S-A-W	Target? Y/N
Writing			
Speaking			
Mathematics			
Science			
Process Types of Basic Skills			
Critical Thinking			
Active Learning			
Learning Strategies			
Monitoring			
Cross-Functional Skills — Those that facilitate performance of activities that occur across jobs			
Social Skills			
Social Perceptiveness			
Coordination			
Persuasion			
Negotiation			
Instructing			
Service Orientation			
Complex Problem Solving Skills			
Complex Problem Solving			
Technical Skills			
Operations Analysis			
Technology Design			

Circle or Highlight Your Skill	Like/Don't Like	S-A-W	Target? Y/N
Equipment Selection			
Installation			
Programming			
Operation Monitoring			
Operation and Control			
Equipment Maintenance			
Troubleshooting			
Repairing			
Quality Control Analysis			
Systems Skills			
Judgment and Decision Making			
Systems Analysis			
Systems Evaluation			

Now take a few minutes and summarize your skills. Which are the your strongest skills that you would like to use in your next job or in your career? (Don't forget to record this in your documentation.) _____

_____

_____

_____

_____

_____

_____

_____

_____

_____

_____

Knowledge

That's gives you an introduction to the "Knowledge" aspect of jobs as opposed to the Skills or anything else you bring to the job search. In the workbook, the job knowledge categories are listed, and it is suggested that you investigate these categories a little to improve your understanding of them. You might have more knowledge than you realize!
Knowledge, as defined by the Department of Labor and O*NET, is "organized sets of principles and facts applying in general domains."

In the second column rate yourself on each item, on a scale of 1 to 5, where 1 is "not really, 3 is "yeah I've got about an average amount", and 5 is "outstanding, top-notch, I really have that knowledge." You could also use Hi, Medium, Lo, or None. Or something like those informal standards. If you are not sure, go the O*NET website and poke around awhile. Look for jobs in each category and then at jobs in the various levels of those categories. Invest the time to understand yourself in the job context. There are no right or wrong answers. It is to your advantage to have a good handle on your Knowledge as it relates to jobs and careers. Use the third column to indicate if you like using that knowledge, a simple "Y" for "Yes" and "N" for "No" works fine. Use the fourth column to indicate with a "Y" or "N" if you might want to accumulate more of that kind of knowledge, through school, training, or on-the-job.

	Rating	Like (Y/N)	More (Y/N)
Administration and Management — Knowledge of business and management principles involved in strategic planning, resource allocation, human resources modeling, leadership technique, production methods, and coordination of people and resources.			
Biology — Knowledge of plant and animal organisms, their tissues, cells, functions, interdependencies, and interactions with each other and the environment.			
Building and Construction — Knowledge of materials, methods, and the tools involved in the construction or repair of houses, buildings, or other structures such as highways and roads.			
Chemistry — Knowledge of the chemical composition, structure, and properties of substances and of the chemical processes and transformations that they undergo. This includes uses of chemicals and their interactions, danger signs, production techniques, and disposal methods.			

	Rating	Like (Y/N)	More (Y/N)
Clerical — Knowledge of administrative and clerical procedures and systems such as word processing, managing files and records, stenography and transcription, designing forms, and other office procedures and terminology.			
Communications and Media — Knowledge of media production, communication, and dissemination techniques and methods. This includes alternative ways to inform and entertain via written, oral, and visual media.			
Computers and Electronics — Knowledge of circuit boards, processors, chips, electronic equipment, and computer hardware and software, including applications and programming.			
Customer and Personal Service — Knowledge of principles and processes for providing customer and personal services. This includes customer needs assessment, meeting quality standards for services, and evaluation of customer satisfaction.			
Design — Knowledge of design techniques, tools, and principles involved in production of precision technical plans, blueprints, drawings, and models.			
Economics and Accounting — Knowledge of economic and accounting principles and practices, the financial markets, banking and the analysis and reporting of financial data.			
Education and Training — Knowledge of principles and methods for curriculum and training design, teaching and instruction for individuals and groups, and the measurement of training effects.			
Engineering and Technology — Knowledge of the practical application of engineering science and technology. This includes applying principles, techniques, procedures, and equipment to the design and production of various goods and services.			

	Rating	Like (Y/N)	More (Y/N)
English Language — Knowledge of the structure and content of the English language including the meaning and spelling of words, rules of composition, and grammar.			
Fine Arts — Knowledge of the theory and techniques required to compose, produce, and perform works of music, dance, visual arts, drama, and sculpture.			
Food Production — Knowledge of techniques and equipment for planting, growing, and harvesting food products (both plant and animal) for consumption, including storage/handling techniques.			
Foreign Language — Knowledge of the structure and content of a foreign (non-English) language including the meaning and spelling of words, rules of composition and grammar, and pronunciation.			
Geography — Knowledge of principles and methods for describing the features of land, sea, and air masses, including their physical characteristics, locations, interrelationships, and distribution of plant, animal, and human life.			
History and Archeology — Knowledge of historical events and their causes, indicators, and effects on civilizations and cultures.			
Law and Government — Knowledge of laws, legal codes, court procedures, precedents, government regulations, executive orders, agency rules, and the democratic political process.			
Mathematics — Knowledge of arithmetic, algebra, geometry, calculus, statistics, and their applications.			
Mechanical — Knowledge of machines and tools, including their designs, uses, repair, and maintenance.			

	Rating	Like (Y/N)	More (Y/N)
Medicine and Dentistry — Knowledge of the information and techniques needed to diagnose and treat human injuries, diseases, and deformities. This includes symptoms, treatment alternatives, drug properties and interactions, and preventive health-care measures.			
Personnel and Human Resources — Knowledge of principles and procedures for personnel recruitment, selection, training, compensation and benefits, labor relations and negotiation, and personnel information systems.			
Philosophy and Theology — Knowledge of different philosophical systems and religions. This includes their basic principles, values, ethics, ways of thinking, customs, practices, and their impact on human culture.			
Physics — Knowledge and prediction of physical principles, laws, their interrelationships, and applications to understanding fluid, material, and atmospheric dynamics, and mechanical, electrical, atomic and sub- atomic structures and processes.			
Production and Processing — Knowledge of raw materials, production processes, quality control, costs, and other techniques for maximizing the effective manufacture and distribution of goods.			
Psychology — Knowledge of human behavior and performance; individual differences in ability, personality, and interests; learning and motivation; psychological research methods; and the assessment and treatment of behavioral and affective disorders.			
Public Safety and Security — Knowledge of relevant equipment, policies, procedures, and strategies to promote effective local, state, or national security operations for the protection of people, data, property, and institutions.			

	Rating	Like (Y/N)	More (Y/N)
Sales and Marketing — Knowledge of principles and methods for showing, promoting, and selling products or services. This includes marketing strategy and tactics, product demonstration, sales techniques, and sales control systems.			
Sociology and Anthropology — Knowledge of group behavior and dynamics, societal trends and influences, human migrations, ethnicity, cultures and their history and origins.			
Telecommunications — Knowledge of transmission, broadcasting, switching, control, and operation of telecommunications systems.			
Therapy and Counseling — Knowledge of principles, methods, and procedures for diagnosis, treatment, and rehabilitation of physical and mental dysfunctions, and for career counseling and guidance.			
Transportation — Knowledge of principles and methods for moving people or goods by air, rail, sea, or road, including the relative costs and benefits.			

Now take a few minutes and summarize your knowledge. Which is your strongest area that you would like to use in your next job or in your career? (Don't forget to record this in your documentation.) _____

_____

_____

Tools & Technology

None of this is section is referenced in the "It's Your Future" book, it is all Bonus Material.

Suppose you had a list of all the different kinds of tools and technology that the U. S. Dept. of Labor had listed in the O*NET on line resource. Suppose further that you could enter the tool and equipment you are familiar with, good at using, and then find jobs and careers that use those tools. Would that help you in identifying jobs and careers you might like have? You bet it would.

Using the O*NET online program, you can enter the name of a tool or technology and get that list of jobs. They are even organized for you! The problem is, you have to know which tools and technology to enter in the search box.

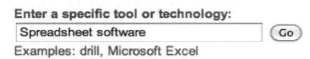

Figure 1 - 1: O*NET OnLine system, Tools & Technology Search screen.

If you had entered that search criteria, this is what the beginning of what the search results would look like:

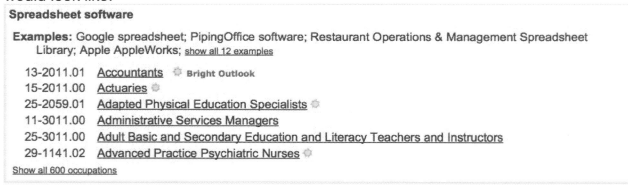

Figure 1 - 2 O*NET OnLine search results for "Spreadsheet software" search criteria.

In fact the complete results are on the following pages:

Music or sound editing software

Examples: Audio editing software; Avid software; Digidesign Pro Tools software; Komplete software; show all 25 examples

- 25-1121.00 Art, Drama, and Music Teachers, Postsecondary
- 25-1122.00 Communications Teachers, Postsecondary
- 11-3021.00 Computer and Information Systems Managers
- 27-2012.02 Directors- Stage, Motion Pictures, Television, and Radio
- 25-1123.00 English Language and Literature Teachers, Postsecondary
- 27-4032.00 Film and Video Editors

Show all 19 occupations

Pattern design software

Examples: Block diagram software; Diagramming software; Flow chart software; Flowchart software; show all 13 examples

- 17-3011.01 Architectural Drafters
- 17-2031.00 Biomedical Engineers
- 17-2061.00 Computer Hardware Engineers
- 15-1143.00 Computer Network Architects
- 15-1121.00 Computer Systems Analysts
- 15-1199.09 Information Technology Project Managers

Show all 10 occupations

Graphics or photo imaging software

Examples: 3D graphic design software; 3D graphics software; Adobe Systems Adobe Photoshop software; Animation software; show all 234 examples

- 25-3011.00 Adult Basic and Secondary Education and Literacy Teachers and Instructors
- 11-2011.00 Advertising and Promotions Managers
- 17-2011.00 Aerospace Engineers
- 17-2021.00 Agricultural Engineers
- 45-2011.00 Agricultural Inspectors
- 19-3091.01 Anthropologists

Show all 197 occupations

Human resources software

Examples: Apex Business Software iBenefits; Apex Business Software iHR; Applicant Tracking Systems ATS software; BEMAS Benefit Management Software; show all 262 examples

- 13-2011.01 Accountants
- 11-3011.00 Administrative Services Managers
- 13-2031.00 Budget Analysts
- 11-1011.00 Chief Executives
- 11-3111.00 Compensation and Benefits Managers
- 13-1141.00 Compensation, Benefits, and Job Analysis Specialists

Show all 34 occupations

Materials requirements planning logistics and supply chain software

Examples: ABB Production Planning software; Aldata G.O.L.D. software; Amber Road software; Applied Software Technologies Asset Maintenance and Materials Management System; show all 172 examples

- 11-9041.00 Architectural and Engineering Managers
- 17-3011.01 Architectural Drafters
- 51-3011.00 Bakers
- 35-1011.00 Chefs and Head Cooks
- 17-3011.02 Civil Drafters
- 35-2014.00 Cooks, Restaurant

Show all 37 occupations

Project management software

Examples: AEC Software FastTrack Schedule for Windows; American Glazing Software AGS WindowPricer; App Software Associations AppTrak.net; Application Software SHEAR; show all 198 examples

- 11-3011.00 Administrative Services Managers
- 11-2011.00 Advertising and Promotions Managers
- 17-2011.00 Aerospace Engineers
- 11-9013.03 Aquacultural Managers
- 17-1011.00 Architects, Except Landscape and Naval
- 11-9041.00 Architectural and Engineering Managers

Show all 200 occupations

Tax preparation software

Examples: Abacus Tax Software; GreatTax software; H&R Block TaxCut Software; Income tax return preparation software; show all 40 examples

- 13-2011.01 Accountants
- 13-1011.00 Agents and Business Managers of Artists, Performers, and Athletes
- 13-2021.01 Assessors
- 11-9199.02 Compliance Managers
- 13-2082.00 Tax Preparers

Financial analysis software

Examples: ACL Business Assurance Analytics software; Accounting fraud detection software; Amortization loan software; AnalyzerXL software; show all 361 examples

- 13-2011.01 Accountants
- 15-2011.00 Actuaries
- 13-2021.02 Appraisers, Real Estate
- 13-2021.01 Assessors
- 13-2011.02 Auditors
- 43-3021.02 Billing, Cost, and Rate Clerks

Show all 53 occupations

Time accounting software

Examples: Automated payroll software; Automated timekeeping software; Blumenthal Software PBSW24; Data Management TimeClock Plus software; show all 84 examples

- 13-2011.01 Accountants
- 11-9013.03 Aquacultural Managers
- 17-1011.00 Architects, Except Landscape and Naval
- 11-9041.00 Architectural and Engineering Managers
- 13-2011.02 Auditors
- 53-6031.00 Automotive and Watercraft Service Attendants

Show all 62 occupations

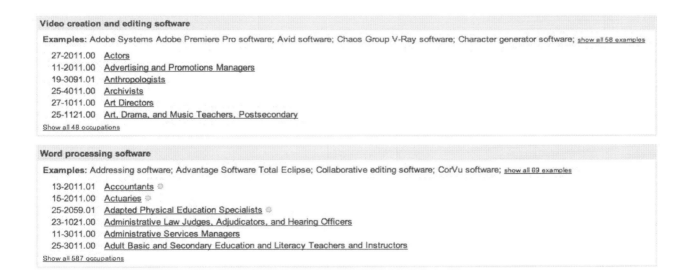

Inventory management software

Examples: AIM Asset Management Software; AJV Food & Beverage software; Argos Software ABECAS Insight WMS; Army Food Management Information System software; show all 75 examples

- 13-2011.01 Accountants
- 17-3021.00 Aerospace Engineering and Operations Technicians
- 49-3011.00 Aircraft Mechanics and Service Technicians
- 11-9041.00 Architectural and Engineering Managers
- 53-6031.00 Automotive and Watercraft Service Attendants
- 49-3021.00 Automotive Body and Related Repairers

Show all 92 occupations

Label making software

Examples: Barcode labeling software; Label printing software; Label-making software; Labeling software; show all 11 examples

- 29-2011.03 Histotechnologists and Histologic Technicians
- 51-9061.00 Inspectors, Testers, Sorters, Samplers, and Weighers
- 17-3029.09 Manufacturing Production Technicians
- 29-1199.04 Naturopathic Physicians
- 51-9111.00 Packaging and Filling Machine Operators and Tenders
- 29-1051.00 Pharmacists

Show all 12 occupations

Expert system software

Examples: Bill review software; Commercial Pro software; Computer aided dispatching auto routing software; Computer assisted telephone interviewing CATI software; show all 45 examples

- 53-2021.00 Air Traffic Controllers
- 13-1031.01 Claims Examiners, Property and Casualty Insurance
- 13-1051.00 Cost Estimators
- 43-5032.00 Dispatchers, Except Police, Fire, and Ambulance
- 13-2051.00 Financial Analysts
- 45-1011.08 First-Line Supervisors of Animal Husbandry and Animal Care Workers

Show all 17 occupations

Video creation and editing software

Examples: Adobe Systems Adobe Premiere Pro software; Avid software; Chaos Group V-Ray software; Character generator software; show all 58 examples

- 27-2011.00 Actors
- 11-2011.00 Advertising and Promotions Managers
- 19-3091.01 Anthropologists
- 25-4011.00 Archivists
- 27-1011.00 Art Directors
- 25-1121.00 Art, Drama, and Music Teachers, Postsecondary

Show all 48 occupations

Word processing software

Examples: Addressing software; Advantage Software Total Eclipse; Collaborative editing software; CorVu software; show all 69 examples

- 13-2011.01 Accountants
- 15-2011.00 Actuaries
- 25-2059.01 Adapted Physical Education Specialists
- 23-1021.00 Administrative Law Judges, Adjudicators, and Hearing Officers
- 11-3011.00 Administrative Services Managers
- 25-3011.00 Adult Basic and Secondary Education and Literacy Teachers and Instructors

Show all 587 occupations

In the next 30+ pages is a list of all of the generic tools and technology that are in the databases that O*NET uses (as of October 2014). You can enter specific tools by brand name, like Microsoft Spreadsheet Software or even Microsoft Excel. However by using the more generic search criteria you increase the number of potential job and career opportunities for you to consider. There are almost 3,000 generic Tool or Technology items listed but almost 44,000 when more specific identifiers are used (like brand names). So, in the interest of brevity, we'll stick with the generics.

You should look through the entire list, maybe highlight all the items you have experience with or like working with. Then go back and from you list of highlighted items, begin your search.

The list, in three columns format:

Abdominal binders
Abdominal retractors
Abrasion testers
Abrasive drums
Abrasive stones
Absorbent booms
Accelerometers
Access servers
Access software
Accounting machines
Accounting software
Acoustic sensors
Acoustic testing rooms
Action games
Acute care fetal or maternal monitoring units or accessories
Adaptive communication switches for the physically challenged
Adding machines
Adhesive rollers
Adjustable forks
Adjustable widemouth pliers
Adjustable wrenches
Administration software
Adult or pediatric intensive care ventilators
Aerial cameras
Aerospace cockpit display panels
Aerospace head up display HUDs
Aging ovens
Aggregate spreaders
Agricultural rollers
Agricultural tractors
Air bags for loading
Air brushes
Air compressors
Air conditioners
Air conveyors
Air dryers
Air exhausters
Air filters

Air manifolds
Air or gas tanks or cylinders
Air pollutant samplers
Air pumps
Air rifles or air handguns
Air samplers or collectors
Air sampling pumps
Air scrubbers
Air velocity and temperature monitors
Aircraft anti skid controls
Aircraft braking systems
Aircraft communication systems
Aircraft cooling fans
Aircraft deicing equipment
Aircraft drag chutes
Aircraft engine compressors
Aircraft environment controllers
Aircraft environment regulators
Aircraft escape or ejection systems
Aircraft fire control or extinguishing systems
Aircraft flight simulators or trainers
Aircraft fuel management systems
Aircraft guidance systems
Aircraft hydraulic systems
Aircraft navigation beacons
Aircraft onboard defrosting or defogging systems
Aircraft oxygen equipment
Aircraft power supply units
Aircraft pushback or tow tractors
Aircraft steering controls
Aircraft warning systems
Airline ticket or boarding pass ATB printers
Alarm systems
Albuminometers

Alcohol analyzers
Alignment jig
All terrain cranes
All terrain vehicles tracked or wheeled
Alternating current or direct current AC DC motors
Amalgam carriers
Ambulances
Amino acid analyzers
Ammeters
Ammonia removal equipment
Amplifiers
Ampoule filling equipment
Amputation retractors
Anaerobic chamber
Anaerobic jars or accessories
Analgesic infusion sets or kits
Analytical balances
Analytical or scientific software
Anatomical human models for medical education or training
Anchor chocks
Anchor lines
Anchor rollers
Anchor setting tools
Anechoic chambers
Anemometers
Anesthesia inhalers or inhaler units or accessories
Anesthesia sets or kits
Angiography contrast medium delivery sets
Angioplasty balloons
Angioscopes or accessories
Angle brackets
Animal catching devices
Animal husbandry equipment

Animal shearing or clipping equipment
Animal watering machines
Animal weighing scales
Anoscopes or proctoscopes
Anti shock garments
Anti static floor mats
Antistatic maintenance kits
Antistatic wrist straps
Anvils
Apnea monitors or accessories
Application server software
Applicator brushes
Arbors
Arc lamps
Archery bows
Arm orthopedic soft goods
Arm traction supplies
Arterial blood gas monitors or accessories
Arterial line catheters
Arterial needles
Articulating boom lift
Artificial airway holders
Asphalt finishers
Assistive listening devices
Atomic absorption AA spectrometers
Atomizers
Attachments or replacement parts for dental instruments
Attenuators
Audio mixing consoles
Audioconferencing systems
Audiometers or accessories
Audiometric bone vibrators or middle ear analyzers
Audiometric booths or acoustic hearing test chambers
Auditory function screening units
Augers
Aural probes
Authentication server software
Autodialers

Automated attendant systems
Automated cover slipping equipment
Automated external defibrillators AED or hard paddles
Automated microscope stages
Automatic call distributor ACD
Automatic pool cleaner
Automatic teller machines ATMs
Automobiles or cars
Automotive cleaners
Automotive doors
Automotive exhaust emission analyzers
Automotive hydraulic systems
Autopsy chisels or osteotomes
Autopsy dissection forceps for general use
Autopsy fluid collection vacuum aspirators or tubing
Autopsy hanging scales
Autopsy knives or blades
Autopsy saws
Autopsy scissors
Autopsy specimen bags or containers
Autosamplers
Autotransfusion units
Aviation ground support software
Awls
Axes
Back or lumbar or sacral orthopedic soft goods
Backhoe boom or boom sections
Backhoes
Backup or archival software
Bacteria transformation kits
Bacterial removal equipment
Bag tag printer

Balance beams or boards or bolsters or rockers for rehabilitation or therapy
Balance or gross motor equipment
Ball valves
Bandage scissors or its supplies
Banders
Bands for dental matrix
Bandsaw wheel
Bar code labels
Bar code reader equipment
Bar coding software
Bar or rod cutters
Bare printed circuit boards
Barometers
Barricades
Baseball bats
Baseballs
Basket stretchers or accessories
Basketballs
Batching plants or feeders
Bath robes
Battery acid hydrometers
Battery chargers
Battery testers
Bead accessories
Bearing fitting tool kits
Bedpans for general use
Bedside pulmonary function screeners
Bells
Below the hook device
Belt conveyors
Bench dog
Bench refractometers or polarimeters
Bench scales
Bench vises
Benchtop centrifuges
Bending machines
Beta counters
Beta gamma counters
Beta gauge measuring systems
Bevels
Bi distillation units

Bi metallic sensors
Bicycles
Binocular light compound microscopes
Binocular vision test sets or accessories
Binoculars
Biological evidence collection kits
Biometric identification equipment
Biopsy needles
Biscuit jointers
Bituminous material distributors
Blades or tooth or other cutting edges
Blanching machinery
Blanket frames or lifters
Blast freezers
Blaster tools
Blocks or pulleys
Blood bank analyzers
Blood bank cell washers
Blood collection needle holders
Blood collection needles
Blood collection syringes
Blood gas analyzers
Blood pressure cuff kits
Blood pressure measuring instrument accessories
Blood pressure recording units
Blood recovery and delivery systems
Blood transfusion filters or screens or accessories
Blood warming or transfusion systems
Blotting or transfer apparatus
Blow molding machines
Blow pipes
Blow torches
Blowers
Board games
Boat Trailer
Body armor

Body bags
Body plethysmographs
Bodyweight measuring scales
Boiler or Heater Ignitor
Bolt cutters
Bone dust collectors
Boom bolters
Borescope inspection equipment
Boring machines
Boring or sinking machinery
Boring tools
Bowling equipment
Box end wrenches
Box sealing tape dispensers
Braces
Brachytherapy units
Braille devices for the physically challenged
Brake repair kits
Breast pumps or its accessories
Breathing circuit bags
Bridge cranes
Bridles
Broaching tools
Broadcast spreaders
Bronchoscopes or accessories
Brooms
Bubble columns
Bucket conveyors
Building blocks
Bulk material carriers
Bulk transporters
Bullet proof vests
Bundling machines
Burners
Busses
Butterfly needles
C clamps
Cable accessories
Cable clamps
Cable reels
Cable splicing kits
Cadaver lifter or transfer devices
Cages or its accessories

Calcium hydroxide placement tools
Calculators or accessories
Calendar and scheduling software
Calendars
Calibrated inductance coils or boxes
Calibrated resistance measuring equipment
Calibration weights or weight sets
Calipers
Calorimeters
Camera based vision systems for automated data collection
Camera controllers
Camera lenses or filters
Canes or cane accessories
Canoes or kayaks
Capacitance meters
Capillary or hematocrit tubes
Cappuccino or espresso machines
Car seats
Carbon filtration equipment
Carbonated beverage dispenser
Card tables
Cardiac output CO monitoring units or accessories
Cardiac pacemaker generators or implantable defibrillators or accessories
Cardiac ultrasound or doppler or echo units or cardioscopes
Cardiopulmonary resuscitation CPR protective shields or masks
Cardiovascular implants
Cardiovascular or thoracic retractors
Cardiovascular sheath kits
Cargo handling equipment
Cargo or container ships

Cargo trucks
Carpet cleaning equipment
Carriages or perambulators or strollers
Carts
Carving tools
Cash or ticket boxes
Cash registers
Cassette players or recorders
Cast cutters or saws
Cast or splint carts
Cast vacuums
Casting machines
Catalytic combustion analyzers
Catalytic converters
Categorization or classification software
Cathode ray tube CRT monitors
Caulking guns
Cell scrapers
Cement bulk material equipment
Cement pumping units
Cement retainers
Central processing unit
CPU processors
Central venous catheters
Centrex phone consoles
Centrifugal compressors
Centrifugal pumps
Centrifugal separation equipment or parts or screens
Centrifuge tubes
Ceramic crucibles
Cervical collars or neck braces
Cervical retractors
Chain conveyors
Chalk lines
Chart projectors or accessories
Chart recorders
Charting software
Check endorsing machines
Check writing machines

Chemical absorption gas analyzers
Chemical or gas sterilizers
Chemical pumps
Chemical tanks
Chemical test strips or papers
Chemiluminescence or bioluminescence analyzers
Chemistry analyzers
Chemistry test kits or supplies
Chest cuirass products
Chest percussors
Childrens science kits
Chilling units or cold water circulators
Chip Spreaders
Chlorine handling equipment
Chopping machinery
Chromatographic detectors
Chromatographic scanners
Chromatography syringes
Chromatography tubing
Chucks
Cinch rescue loops
Cinematographic cameras
Circuit breakers
Circuit tester
Circuit tracers
Circulating baths
Circulation heaters
Clamp On Multimeter
Clay or modeling tools
Cleaning brushes
Cleaning dusters
Cleaning machines for seed or grain or dried leguminous vegetables
Cleaning scrapers
Climbing devices for rehabilitation or therapy
Clinical hydraulic lifts or accessories
Clinical incubators or infant warmers
Clinical trapeze bars
Clinometers

Clock timers
Clothes dryers
Clustering software
Coagulation analyzers
Cocktail shakers or accessories
Cognitive or dexterity or perceptual or sensory evaluation or testing products
Cognitive toys
Coiled tubing injector heads
Coiled tubing units
Coin banks
Coin sorters
Coin wrapper machines
Cold chisels
Cold forming presses
Cold planers
Coliwasas
Collection tanks
Color perception testing lanterns
Color sensors
Colorimeters
Colposcopes or vaginoscopes or accessories
Combination furniture sets for dental procedures
Combination refractor keratometers
Combination wrenches
Combine harvesters
Combustible or hazardous gas detectors for power generators
Commercial fishing nets
Commercial passenger propeller aircraft
Commercial use barbeque ovens
Commercial use blenders
Commercial use broilers
Commercial use coffee grinders
Commercial use coffee or iced tea makers

Commercial use convection ovens

Commercial use conveyer toasters

Commercial use cotton candy machines or accessories

Commercial use cutlery

Commercial use deep fryers

Commercial use dishwashers

Commercial use dough machines

Commercial use electric can openers

Commercial use food choppers or cubers or dicers

Commercial use food grinders

Commercial use food processors

Commercial use food slicers

Commercial use food warmers

Commercial use graters

Commercial use griddles

Commercial use grills

Commercial use heat lamps

Commercial use high pressure steamers

Commercial use hot dog grills

Commercial use icing sets or bags

Commercial use juicers

Commercial use measuring cups

Commercial use microwave ovens

Commercial use mixers

Commercial use molds

Commercial use ovens

Commercial use pasta cookers

Commercial use pasta machines

Commercial use peelers

Commercial use pizza ovens

Commercial use popcorn machines

Commercial use ranges

Commercial use rice cookers

Commercial use rolling pins

Commercial use rotisseries

Commercial use scales

Commercial use smokers or smoke ovens

Commercial use steamers

Commercial use strainers

Commercial use toasters

Commercial use waffle irons

Commercial use woks

Commercial water heaters

Commodity Title

Compact disc CD or labeling printers

Compact disk players or recorders

Compact disks CDs

Compactors

Comparators

Compasses

Compiler and decompiler software

Complementary deoxyribonucleic acid cDNA synthesis kits

Completion hydraulic pumps

Complex controlling devices

Compliance software

Composite placement tools

Composter

Compressed air gun

Compression testers

Computed tomography CT or CAT radiotherapy simulators

Computer aided design CAD software

Computer aided manufacturing CAM software

Computer based training software

Computer display glare screens

Computer mouse or trackballs

Computer servers

Computer tool kits

Concrete mixers or plants

Concrete or cement testing instruments

Concrete paving strike offs

Concrete spreaders

Concrete vibrators

Condensing units

Conductivity cells

Conductivity meters

Conduit benders

Configuration management software

Contact center software

Container trailers

Content delivery networking equipment

Content workflow software

Continuous arteriovenous dialysis CAVHD units or related products

Continuous mining equipment

Continuous passive motion CPM devices or accessories

Control valves

Conventional truck cranes

Conversation recording units

Convex security mirrors

Conveyor feeders

Conveyor rails

Conveyor roller

Conveyor screw

Cooking machinery

Cool containers

Coordinate measuring machines CMM

Core drills

Core drying ovens

Coring equipment

Corneal topographers
Corona treaters
Coronary stents
Corrosion testers
Cosmetic dentistry curing lights or accessories
Costumes or accessories
Coulometers
Counterbores
Counters
Countersinks
Creep testers
Crochet hooks
Crop dividers
Croquet sets
Cross cut chisels
Cross trainers
Crown or bridge removers
Crucible furnaces
Crucibles for dental casting machines
Cruise ships
Crushers
Crushing machinery
Crutches or crutch accessories
Cryogenic or liquid nitrogen freezers
Cryogenic temperature controllers
Cryostats
Cryosurgery equipment or accessories
Crystal growing equipment
Crystallizers
Cultivators
Culture tubes
Curbing machines
Curing machines
Curves
Customer relationship management CRM software
Cutlery or utensils for the physically challenged
Cutting dies or tooling
Cutting machinery
Cutting machines
Cutting or paring boards for the physically challenged

Cuvettes
Cyclone or vortex grinders
Cystourethroscopes
Dam
Darkfield microscopes
Data base management system software
Data base reporting software
Data base user interface and query software
Data compression software
Data conversion software
Data mining software
Deburring equipment
Decontamination shower
Decorticators
Defense Digital Imaging Network DIN system equipment
Deflecting devices
Dehumidifiers
Dehydrating machinery
Dehydrators
Deionization or demineralization equipment
Delivery trucks
Demolition equipment kits
Demolition hammers
Densitometers
Density gradient fractionators
Dental absorbent holders
Dental amalgam carvers
Dental amalgamators
Dental anesthesia sets or accessories
Dental articulators or accessories
Dental bite blocks or wings or tabs
Dental burnishers
Dental burs
Dental calipers
Dental cord packers
Dental cryosurgical units
Dental cutting or separating discs
Dental dam supplies

Dental dehydrators
Dental depth gauges
Dental drills or drill bits
Dental elevators
Dental examination chairs or related parts or accessories
Dental excavators
Dental files or rasps
Dental filler contouring instruments
Dental film processors
Dental finishing or polishing discs
Dental finishing or polishing kits
Dental forceps
Dental formers
Dental gages or accessories
Dental hand pieces or accessories
Dental hygiene instruments
Dental impression material syringes or accessories
Dental impression material water baths or accessories
Dental impression trays
Dental instrument sharpening accessories
Dental knives
Dental laboratory air abrasion units
Dental laboratory burners or torches
Dental laboratory casting machines or its parts or accessories
Dental laboratory curing units
Dental laboratory dies
Dental laboratory dust collectors
Dental laboratory flasks
Dental laboratory furnaces
Dental laboratory gold platers or supplies
Dental laboratory lathes or accessories

Dental laboratory model trimmers or accessories
Dental laboratory plaster traps
Dental laboratory sandblasters or supplies
Dental laboratory soldering machines or supplies
Dental laboratory vacuum units or supplies
Dental laboratory vibrators
Dental laboratory waxing units
Dental lasers
Dental mallets
Dental margin trimmers
Dental marking devices
Dental material pluggers or tips or accessories
Dental materials dispensers
Dental matrices or sets
Dental mirrors or mirror handles
Dental mouth props
Dental nippers
Dental obturating points
Dental operatory retraction cords
Dental pin drivers
Dental placement instruments
Dental plaster knives
Dental pressure indicating kits
Dental probes
Dental prophylaxis kits
Dental pulp or vitality testers
Dental radiology film
Dental reamers
Dental retainers
Dental retractors
Dental root tip picks
Dental saliva ejectors or oral suction devices or supplies
Dental scalers or accessories
Dental scissors
Dental shades

Dental spatulas
Dental spreaders
Dental stones
Dental syringe accessory kits
Dental syringes or needles or syringes with needles
Dental tongs
Dental tooth separators
Dental tweezers
Dental wax carvers
Dental wedges or sets
Dental x ray apparatus parts or kits or accessories
Dental x ray units
Deoxyribonucleic sequence analyzers
Depth gauges
Depth indicators
Depth perception apparatus
Derricks
Desktop communications software
Desktop computers
Desktop publishing software
Detection apparatus for non metallic objects
Detonators
Developing tanks
Development environment software
Device drivers or system software
Dewatering equipment
Dewatering pumps
Diagnostic or interventional vascular catheter introducers or sets
Diagnostic or interventional vascular catheters or sets
Diagonal cut pliers
Dial calibrated intravenous flowmeters or regulators
Diaphragm pumps
Dibblers
Dice
Dictation machines
Die bends
Diesel engines

Diesel freight locomotives
Diesel generators
Diesel passenger locomotives
Diffractometers
Digestion systems
Digging bars
Digital camcorders or video cameras
Digital cameras
Digital duplicators
Digital image printers
Digital Imaging Communications in Medicine DICOM standard system equipment
Digital readout recorders
Digital Signal Processor DSP
Digital Telephones
Digital testers
Digital video disk players or recorders
Digital voice recorders
Direct current DC motors
Direction finding compasses
Dish drainer
Disks
Dissection kits or supplies
Dissolution or disintegration testers
Dissolved carbon dioxide analyzers
Dissolved oxygen meters
Distance meters
Distillation pipings or columns or fittings
Ditchers
Diving instruments or accessories
Dock plates
Dock ramps
Document camera
Document management software
Doll houses
Dollies
Dolls
Domestic apple corer

Domestic clothes washers
Domestic clothing irons
Domestic coffee makers
Domestic dish washers
Domestic double boilers
Domestic electric knives
Domestic electric skillets
Domestic garbage disposals
Domestic garlic press
Domestic garnishing tools
Domestic kitchen funnels
Domestic kitchen or food thermometers
Domestic kitchen tongs
Domestic knife sharpeners
Domestic knives
Domestic melon or butter baller
Domestic microwave ovens
Domestic mist or trigger sprayers
Domestic ranges
Domestic sewing machines
Domestic sifter
Domestic strainers or colanders
Domestic toaster ovens
Domestic trash compactors
Domestic tumble dryers
Domestic vegetable brush
Domestic whipped cream maker
Domestic wooden oven paddle
Door openers
Dosimeters
Dot matrix printers
Downhole fishing poles
Drafting kits or sets
Draglines
Drain or pipe cleaning equipment
Drain or toilet plunger
Dredgers
Dressing sticks for the physically challenged
Drill bits
Drilling machines
Dropping pipettes

Drug delivery systems or accessories
Drum grabs
Drums
Dry baths or heating blocks
Dry erase boards or accessories
Dry heat or hot air sterilizers
Dry wall single chamber carbon dioxide incubators
Drying cabinets or ovens
Ductility testing machines
Dump trucks
Dust collectors
Dust mops
Dusters
Dye sublimation printers
Dynamometers
Ear muffs
Ear plugs
Ear retractors
Earthmoving buckets or its parts or accessories
Earthmoving shovels
Eddy current examination equipment
Edgers
Edging tools
Egg inspection or collecting equipment
Electric boilers
Electric downhole pumps
Electric freight locomotives
Electric passenger locomotives
Electric vibrators for rehabilitation or therapy
Electrical frequency meters
Electrical inductance sensors
Electrical insulators
Electrical or power regulators
Electrical power sensors
Electrical resistance or conductance sensors
Electro pneumatic transducers

Electrocardiography EKG accessories
Electrocardiography EKG patch electrodes
Electrocardiography EKG transmitter or telemetry or accessories
Electrocardiography EKG unit analyzers
Electrocardiography EKG units
Electrocochleographs
Electrode holders
Electroencephalography EEG units or accessories
Electrogravimetry analyzers
Electrolyte analyzers
Electromagnetic field meters
Electromagnetic geophysical instruments
Electromagnets
Electrometers
Electromyographs
Electromyography EMG units or accessories
Electron guns
Electron microscopes
Electronic actuators
Electronic blood pressure units
Electronic charts or maps or atlases
Electronic counters
Electronic encyclopedias
Electronic funds transfer point of sale equipment
Electronic loads
Electronic mail software
Electronic measuring probes
Electronic media or data duplicating equipment
Electronic medical thermometers
Electronic multichannel pipetters
Electronic stethoscopes or accessories

Electronic toploading balances
Electrophoresis system accessories
Electrophoresis system power supplies
Electroporation cuvettes
Electrostatic apparatus
Electrosurgical or electrocautery equipment or accessories or related products
Electrotherapy combination units
Elevating scrapers
Elevators
Embalming cavity injectors
Embalming injecting tubes
Embalming injector needles
Embalming vein drainage tubes
Emergency medical services cervical or extrication collars
Emergency medical services first aid kits
Emergency medical services head immobilizers
Emergency medical services intravenous IV kits
Emergency medical services obstetrics kits
Emergency medical services oxygen or resuscitation kits
Emergency medical services rappel kits
Emergency medical services suction units or accessories
Emergency medical services torso immobilizers
Emergency medical services tourniquets or clamps
Emergency medical services tracheal tube or cricothyrotomy kits

Emergency medical services triage tags
Emergency or resuscitation carts
Emergency response litters or stretchers or accessories
Emergency resuscitator or aspirator kits
Emergency vehicle exits
Encoder decoder equipment
End cut pliers
End tidal carbon dioxide monitors or supplies
Endoscope maintenance units or accessories
Endoscopic clamps or dissectors or graspers or forceps or ligators
Endoscopic cytology or microbiology brushes
Endoscopic dilators or inflation devices or related products
Endoscopic equipment or procedure carts or accessories
Endoscopic equipment sets
Endoscopic instrument packs or trays or kits
Endoscopic instrument sets
Endoscopic insufflation or distention units or accessories
Endoscopic printers or accessories
Endoscopic snares or snare wires or accessories
Endoscopic suction or irrigation tips or coagulation probes or accessories
Endoscopic video cameras or recorders or adapters or accessories
Endoscopic water bottles or accessories
Endotracheal or tracheotomy sets
Endotracheal tubes
Enema kits or accessories

Engine ignition systems
Engine or component test stands
Engine or vehicle stands
Engraving machines
Enteral feeding administration sets
Enteral feeding infusion pump tubing sets
Enterprise application integration software
Enterprise resource planning ERP software
Entomological catching equipment
Enzyme analyzers
Epidiascopes
Epidural trays or accessories
Equalizers
Esophageal tubes
Evaporative coolers
Exercise balls
Exercise trampolines
Exophthalmometers
Expanders
Expert system software
Explosimeters
Explosive initiators
Extendable conveyors
Extension pole
Extensometers
Exterior automobile lighting
Extracting equipment for laboratories
Extremities cradles
Extremity hydrotherapy baths or tanks
Extremity restraints
Extruders
Extruders for modeling materials
Eye bolts
Eye charts or vision cards
Eye occluders
Eye shields
Eyemagnets for ophthalmic surgery

Eyewashers or eye wash stations
Fabric or netting for entomology
Facial shields
Facilities management software
Facsimile machines
Fall protection lanyard
Fans
Fat extractors
Fatigue testers
Feed mixers
Feed or drive rollers
Feeder jig
Feeding bottles or accessories
Feeler gauges
Fertilizer spreaders or distributors
Fetal or gynecological ultrasound or echo units
Fiber optic fault locators
Fiber optic test sources
Fiber sensors
Fids
Field strength measuring equipment
File versioning software
Files
Filesystem software
Filing cabinets or accesories
Filling machinery
Filling or sealing auger dose machines
Film editors
Film projectors
Filter papers
Filtering machinery
Filters or other spare parts for samplers
Financial analysis software
Finger ring removers
Fingerprint applicators or brushes
Fingerprint equipment
Fingerprint latent print kits
Fire blankets

Fire escape equipment
Fire extinguishers
Fire fighting watercraft
Fire hoses or nozzles
Fire or rescue trucks
Fire pump sets
Fire retardant apparel
Fire retardant footwear
Fire suppression hand tools
Fire suppression system
Fire tube boilers
Fish tape
Fishing boats
Fishing reels
Fishing rods
Fitness weights
Fixed screens
Flags or accessories
Flame ionization analyzers
Flare or vent stacks
Flares
Flash memory storage devices
Flashlights
Flask or retort units
Flat nose pliers
Flatbed trailers
Flexible endoscopes or accessories or related products
Flexographic printer
Flexure or transverse testing machines
Flight computer systems
Flight control software
Floats
Floor centrifuges
Floor grade forceps or hemostats
Floor grade nail nippers
Floor grade needle holders
Floor or platform scales
Floor polishers
Floor scrapers
Floor scrubbers
Floor washing machine
Floppy disks
Floppy drives

Flow injection analysis equipment
Flow sensors
Flow sensors or regulators or components
Flow transmitters
Flowmeters
Fluid regulators
Fluorescent lamps
Fluorescent microscopes
Flying insect control traps
Fog or mist generators
Foot care products
Foot switches
Footballs
Footprint lifters
Footwear covers
Force or torque sensors
Forced air or mechanical convection general purpose incubators
Forensic chemical workstations
Forensic magnifiers
Forestry increment borers
Forestry saws
Forestry skidders
Forging presses
Forging tooling
Forklift or elevator accessories or supplies
Forklifts
Form or fill or seal machinery
Form tools or toolbits
Forming machine
Foundry crucibles
Foundry flasks
Foundry ladles
Foundry molds
Fractionation apparatus
Franking or postage machines
Freeze dryers or lyopholizers
Freezedryers or lyophilzers
French pressure cells
Frequency analyzers

Frequency calibrator or simulator
Frequency converters
Frequency counters or timer or dividers
Friction apparatus
Front end loaders
Fuel pumps
Full body immersion hydrotherapy baths or tanks
Full body restraints
Fume hoods or cupboards
Furnaces
Furniture moving discs
Fuse pullers
Gage block set
Gait belts for rehabilitation or therapy
Galvanic or faradic stimulators
Galvanometers
Game pads or joy sticks
Gamma counters
Garden forks
Garment steamer
Gas anesthesia apparatus
Gas burners
Gas chromatographs
Gas detector tubes
Gas detectors
Gas engines
Gas gauges
Gas generators
Gas masks
Gas or vapour concentration measuring instruments
Gas recovery machinery
Gas turbine control panels
Gas welding or brazing or cutting apparatus
Gastric decompression tubes
Gastrointestinal retractors
Gastrostomy feeding tube kits
Gate valves
Gateway software

Gauges or inspection fixtures
Gear cutting tools
Gear pumps
Gear shapers
Geiger counters
Gel boxes
Gel documentation accessories
Gel documentation systems
Gel dryers
Gel filtration equipment
General cloning vectors
General dental lights or its accessories
General purpose refrigerators or refrigerator freezers
General purpose trays
Generator control or protection panels
Geological compasses
Geological prospecting apparatus
Geriatric chairs or accessories
GFI circuit testers
Girder trolleys
Glass crucibles
Glass cutters
Glass injection moldings
Glass tubing
Glass vacuum moldings
Global positioning system receivers
Globe valves
Glucose monitors or meters
Glue guns
Go cart
Go or no go gauge
Goggles
Golf carts
Golf clubs
Goniometers
Grab hooks
Graders
Graders or land levelers
Grading machines for seed

or grain or dried leguminous vegetables
Grain analyzers
Graphic recorders
Graphical user interface development software
Graphics card driver software
Graphics or photo imaging software
Graphics or video accelerator cards
Graphics tablets
Grapples
Gravimeters
Grease fitting
Grease guns
Greenhouse ventilation equipment
Grinders
Grinding machines
Grinding mills
Grinding or polishing machines
Grinding wheel dressers
Grinding wheels
Grip strengthener
Grit blast machines
Grit chambers
Ground power units for aircraft
Grounding devices or assemblies
Grounding hardware
Grouting machines
Guide jig
Guitars
Gurneys or scissor lifts
Gyratory crushers
Gyroscopic instruments
Hair care supplies
Hammer drills
Hammer mills
Hammers
Hand clamps
Hand held camcorders or video cameras
Hand held rock drills

Hand held vascular dopplers or accessories
Hand looms
Hand or body lotions
Hand or finger traction supplies
Hand or push drill
Hand pumps
Hand sewing needles
Hand sprayers
Hand trucks or accessories
Handcuffs
Handguns
Handheld refractometers or polarimeters
Handheld thermometer
Handicraft tools or materials or equipment for the physically challenged
Handrails
Hard disk arrays
Hard disk drives
Hard hats
Hardness testers
Harmonicas
Harnesses or its accessories
Harrows
Harvester parts or accessories
Harvesters
Hatchets
Haymaking machinery
Hazardous material protective apparel
Hazardous material protective footwear
Head or neck traction supplies
Headphones
Headpointers or mouthsticks for the physically challenged
Hearing aid analyzers or test systems
Hearing aids for the physically challenged
Heart and lung machines or accessories

Heat exchangers
Heat guns
Heat pumps
Heat sinks
Heat stress monitors
Heat tracing equipment
Heated walk in environmental or growth chambers
Heater elements
Heating mantles or tapes
Heating or drying equipment or accessories
Hedge clippers
Heel grounding straps
Height gauges
Helpdesk or call center software
Hemacytometer sets
Hematology analyzers
Hematology or chemistry mixers
Hemocytometers
Hemodialysis dialyzer reprocessing systems
Hemodialysis units
HEPA filtered enclosures
Hex keys
Hickeys
High capacity removable media drives
High end computer servers
High frequency ventilators
High pressure liquid chromatograph chromatography
High pressure sodium lamps
High vacuum combustion apparatus
High vacuum equipment
High voltage cable detection
Hipot testers
Histological hones or straps or compounds
Histological knives or knife holders or blades
Histological staining apparatus

Histology or cytology slide stainers
Histology or tissue cassette cabinets
Histology paraffin
Histology sampling and dissecting stations
Histology tissue cassettes
Hoeing machines
Hoes
Hoists
Hold down clamps
Holding fixtures
Hole diggers
Hole saws
Home care ventilators
Homogenizers
Hose cutter
Hospital intercom systems
Hot air blowers
Hot cell remote handling equipment
Hot cell remote viewing device
Human resources software
Humidifiers
Hybridization ovens or incubators
Hydraulic accumulators
Hydraulic cylinder or component repair kits
Hydraulic generators
Hydraulic motors
Hydraulic press frames
Hydraulic pumps
Hydraulic rock drills
Hydraulic truck cranes
Hydrocarbons analyzers or detectors
Hydroelectric engines
Hydrometers
Hydrotherapy bath or tank accessories
Hygrometers
Hypodermic injection apparatus or accessories
Hypodermic needles
Ice cream machines
Ice dispensers

Ice shaver machines or accessories
Identification markers
Illuminators for microscopes
Immersion circulators
Immersion heaters
Immunology analyzers
Immunology or serology quality controls or calibrators or standards
Immunology or serology test kits or supplies
Impact crushers
Impact hammers
Impact testers
Impact wrenches
Impedance meters
Incandescent lamps
Incinerators
Incubator accessories
Incubators or brooders for poultry
Induction dryers
Induction heaters
Inductively coupled plasma ICP spectrometers
Industrial control software
Industrial funnels
Industrial nucleonic moisture measuring systems
Industrial shrink wrap equipment
Infant scales
Information retrieval or search software
Informational signs
Infra red or ultra violet absorption analyzers
Infrared dryers
Infrared imagers
Infrared lamps
Infrared spectrometers
Infusion pump kits or accessories
Injection molding machines
Injectors
Inkjet printers
Inoculating devices

Insertion tools
Instant messaging platform
Instant messaging software
Instant print cameras
Instrument disinfectant washing equipment
Instrument tables for surgical or obstetrical delivery use or accessories or related products
Instrument transformers
Instrument tripods
Instrumentation for capillary electrophoresis
Insulated clothing for cold environments
Insulated or flotation suits
Insulation testers
Intake structures
Integrated circuit testers
Integrated maintenance information systems
Integrated motion control systems
Integrated services digital network ISDN access devices
Integrated services digital network ISDN testers
Integrated tool carriers
Interactive voice recognition equipment
Interactive voice response software
Intercom systems
Interferometers
Intermittent positive pressure breathing IPPB machines
Internet browser software
Internet directory services software
Intraaortic balloon pumps or accessories
Intracranial pressure ICP monitoring units or accessories
Intrauterine catheters or catheterization kits

Intravenous infusion pump analyzers or sensors
Intravenous infusion pumps for general use
Intravenous or arterial administration ports or injection sites or caps or protectors
Intravenous or arterial arm boards
Intravenous or arterial cannulas or accessories
Intravenous or arterial catheter trays
Intravenous or arterial extension tubing
Intravenous or arterial infusion fluid warmers
Intravenous or arterial infusion single port bags or containers
Intravenous or arterial tubing adapters or connectors or locks or caps or protectors
Intravenous or arterial tubing administration sets
Intravenous syringe infusion pumps
Intravenous tubing with catheter administration kits
Introducers or guide pins or guidewires or glidewires for non endoscopic surgical or open heart procedures
Intubation forceps
Intubation gauges or guides
Intubation stylets
Intubator components or accessories
Inventory management software
Inverted microscopes
Ion analyzers
Ion chromatographs
Ion exchange apparatus
Ion exchange equipment
Ion implantation equipment
Ion selective electrode

Ion selective electrode ISE meters
Ionization chambers
Ionmeters
IR 192 radiography examination equipment
Ironing machines or presses
Irradiation gamma sources
Irrigation pipes or tubes
Irrigation pumps
Irrigation trickles
Isolation glove boxes
Isolators
J hooks
Jacks
Jaw crushers
Joint cleaning or refacing machines
Juicing machinery
Jump ropes
Kettle exchangers
Keyboards
Kilns for firing ceramics
Kjeldahl nitrogen determination apparatus
Knee braces or hinged knee supports
Knife blades
Lab coats
Label applying machines
Label dispensers
Label making machines
Label making software
Label making tapes
Laboratory adapters or connectors or fittings
Laboratory animal restraints or harnesses
Laboratory bailers
Laboratory balances
Laboratory beakers
Laboratory benches
Laboratory blenders or emulsifiers
Laboratory box furnaces
Laboratory bridges
Laboratory burets
Laboratory centrifugal pumps

Laboratory chillers
Laboratory clamps
Laboratory cork borers
Laboratory crushers or pulverizers
Laboratory diluters
Laboratory dishes
Laboratory evaporators
Laboratory filtration hardware or accessories
Laboratory flasks
Laboratory forceps
Laboratory freezer or refrigerator thermometers
Laboratory funnels
Laboratory general purpose tubing
Laboratory graduated cylinders
Laboratory heat exchange condensers
Laboratory heaters
Laboratory hotplates
Laboratory incubator thermometers
Laboratory insect containers
Laboratory knives
Laboratory mechanical convection ovens
Laboratory membrane filters
Laboratory microwave ovens
Laboratory mills
Laboratory mixers
Laboratory presses
Laboratory safety furnaces
Laboratory safety ovens
Laboratory scalpels
Laboratory scissors
Laboratory separators
Laboratory sifting equipment
Laboratory spatulas
Laboratory sprayers
Laboratory staining dishes or jars
Laboratory stirring rods
Laboratory tongs
Laboratory tools

Laboratory vacuum pumps
Laboratory vials
Laboratory vibrators
Laboratory washing machines
Lachrymal dilators or sets
Lacing or stringing accessories
Ladders
Laminar flow cabinets or stations
Laminators
LAN software
Lancets
Land drilling rigs
Landing gear assemblies
Lap mayo trays or mayo stands for surgical use or accessories
Laparoscopes or laparoscopic telescopes
Laryngoscopes or accessories
Laser beam analyzers
Laser cutting tools
Laser filters
Laser measuring systems
Laser printers
Laser welding machinery
Lasers
Lathe tools or dies
Lathes
Laundry type washing machines
Lawnmowers
Leak testing equipment
Leather accessories
Ledger paper
Leg orthopedic softgoods or accessories
Leg protectors
Leg traction supplies
Lens measuring equipment
Letter folders
Letter or symbol boards for the physically challenged
Lettering equipment
Letterpress equipment
Level generators

Level meter
Level sensors or transmitters
Levels
Library software
License management software
Life rings
Life vests or preservers
Lifeboats or liferafts
Lifelines or lifeline equipment
Lift stations
Lifter plate
Lifting hooks
Lifts
Light absorption meters
Light bulb changer
Light enhancing cameras or vision devices
Light scattering equipment
Light stylus
Light trucks or sport utility vehicles
Lighters
Lightmeters
Limit switches
Limousines
Linear position sensors
Linemans pliers
Lip retractors
Liquid chromatographs
Liquid chromatography fittings
Liquid crystal display LCD panels or monitors
Liquid crystal display projection panels
Liquid crystal display projector
Liquid leak detectors
Liquid penetrant examination equipment
Liquid scintillation counters
Livestock identification equipment
Livestock trailers
Load frame
Loadcells

Loading equipment
Location based messaging service platforms
Locking pliers
Lockout devices
Logging instruments for water wells
Long term continuous electrocardiography EKG or holter monitoring systems
Longnose pliers
Loudspeakers
Loupes
Low cab forward tractors
Low voltage alternating and direct current AC DC panelboards
Lower body resistance machines
Lower extremity prosthetic devices
Lubricating oil testing kit
Lug crimping tool dies
Lumbering equipment
Lung retractors
Luxmeters
Machetes
Machine end mills
Machine mounts or vibration isolators
Machinery cutting knives or knife assemblies
Macrame accessories
Magnetic card readers
Magnetic particle examination equipment
Magnetic spin bars or stir bars or stirring beads
Magnetic stirrers
Magnetic tape recorders
Magnetic tools
Magnetometer geophysical instruments
Magnetometers
Magnifiers
Mail opening machines
Mail sealing machines
Mainframe computers

Mainframe console or dumb terminals
Makeup kits
Mallets
Manicure implements
Manipulators
Manlift or personnel lift
Manometers
Manostats
Manual multichannel air displacement pipetters
Manual or electronic hematology differential cell counters
Manual resuscitators
Manual single channel air displacement pipetters
Manual single channel positive displacement pipetters
Manual single channel repeating pipetters
Manual wire straighteners
Map creation software
Map measurers
Marine craft communications systems
Marine hatchery equipment
Marine signaling systems
Mask or respirators filters or accessories
Masking equipment
Masks or accessories
Masks or fins or snorkels
Mass spectrometers
Mat cutter
Mat knives
Material handling hoses
Materials requirements planning logistics and supply chain software
Mats or platforms for rehabilitation or therapy
Measuring rods
Measuring tables
Measuring tapes
Measuring wheels for distance
Mechanical balances

Mechanical stethoscopes or accessories
Media control systems
Medical aerosol tents
Medical aspiration or irrigation syringes
Medical bulb syringes
Medical c arm x ray units
Medical charting systems components or accessories
Medical cine fluoroscopy equipment
Medical computed tomography CT or CAT 3 dimensional system components
Medical computed tomography CT or CAT complete stationery unit installations
Medical computed tomography CT or CAT contrast agent injectors
Medical computed tomography CT or CAT quality assurance or calibration phantoms or devices
Medical computed tomography CT or CAT scanners or tubes
Medical diagnostic pinwheels
Medical exam headlights or headlamps or accessories
Medical exam or non surgical procedure gloves
Medical examining mirror headbands or accessories
Medical gamma cameras for general use
Medical gas cylinders or related devices
Medical head hoods
Medical heat lamps or accessories
Medical hydrocollators or accessories

Medical hyperbaric chambers
Medical imaging contrast agent injectors or accessories
Medical imaging dry laser printers or imagers
Medical imaging wet darkroom or daylight processors
Medical incision drainage bags or reservoirs
Medical incision drains
Medical lamps
Medical linear accelerator intensity modulated radiation therapy IMRT collimators
Medical linear accelerator intensity modulated radiation therapy IMRT three dimensional units
Medical linear accelerator intensity modulated radiation therapy IMRT two dimensional units
Medical magnetic resonance imaging MRI 3 dimensional system components
Medical magnetic resonance imaging MRI quality assurance or calibration phantoms or devices
Medical magnetic resonance imaging MRI scanners
Medical nasal cannulae
Medical nasal catheters or catheterization kits
Medical oxygen masks or parts
Medical oxygen tubing or connectors
Medical picture archiving computer systems PACS
Medical positron emission tomography PET units

Medical radiation dosimeters
Medical radiation films or badges
Medical radiographic equipment grids
Medical radioisotope scanners
Medical radiological positioning aids for general radiological use
Medical radiological shielding aprons or masks or drapes
Medical radiological shielding freestanding or portable screens
Medical radiological shielding gloves
Medical radiological shielding portable containers for radioactive materials
Medical radiological shielding wall or ceiling or floor installed panels
Medical single photon emission computed tomography SPECT units
Medical software
Medical staff aprons or bibs
Medical staff coveralls
Medical staff isolation or cover gowns
Medical staff isolation or surgical masks
Medical staff scrubs
Medical staple or clip removers
Medical suction cannulas or tubes or accessories
Medical suction or vacuum appliances
Medical suction sets or kits
Medical syringes with needles
Medical syringes without needles
Medical tape measures

Medical tuning forks
Medical ultrasound bone densitometers
Medical ultrasound or doppler or echo monitors
Medical ultrasound or doppler or echo printers
Medical ultrasound or doppler or echo probes
Medical ultrasound or doppler or echo three dimensional components
Medical ultrasound or doppler or echo transducers or accessories
Medical ultrasound or doppler or pulse echo or echography units for general diagnostic use
Medical x ray apparatus filters
Medical x ray buckys
Medical x ray darkroom equipment or supplies
Medical x ray film archiving system software
Medical x ray film or cassettes for general use
Medical x ray intensifying screens
Medical x ray quality assurance or calibration devices
Medical x ray units for general diagnostic use
Medication or pill dispensers or accessories
Megaphones
Megohmmeters
Melting point recorders
Mercury blood pressure units
Mercury vapor lamps
Metadata management software
Metal cutters
Metal detectors
Metal fabric media

Metal inert gas MIG welding machinery
Metal markers or holders
Metal stamps
Metal stamps or punches
Metal testing instruments
Metallic bins
Metallic glitter
Metallurgical microscopes
Meteorology instrument accessories
Metering pumps
Metronomes
Microbiological aircontrol equipment
Microbiology analyzers
Microbiology fermentation equipment
Microbiology inoculation loops or needles
Microbiology slide stainers
Microcentrifuges
Microcontrollers
Microfiche or microfilm viewer components or accessories
Microfiche or microfilm viewers
Microfiche reader printers
Microfilm cameras
Microfilm processors
Micrometers
Microphones
Microplate readers
Microplate washers
Microplates
Microprocessors
Microscope condensers
Microscope objectives
Microscope slide cabinets
Microscope slide racks
Microscope slides
Microscope stages
Microscopic structure estimation apparatus
Microtomes
Microwave core equipment
Microwave leakage meters
Military rifles

Milk cooling tanks
Milk dispensers
Milking machines
Milkshake machines
Milling cutters
Milling machines
Minibuses
Minivans or vans
Mitre box
Mixers or agitators
Mobile excavators
Mobile location based services software
Mobile messaging service software
Mobile operator specific application software
Mobile or transportable medical linear accelerators
Mobile phones
Modems
Modulation meters
Modulators
Moisture balances
Moisture meters
Molding machines
Money counting machines
Monochromators
Monocular microscopes
Mop wringer
Morgue cabinet refrigerators
Mortuary aspirators
Motherboards
Motor compressors
Motor drive or control integrated circuits
Motor starter controls
Motorcycles
Mountain bicycles
Moving message signs
Mowers
MP3 Players or Recorders
Mud agitators
Mud pumps
Multi function printers
Multi gas monitors
Multichannel intravenous infusion pumps
Multimedia projectors

Multimeters
Multipurpose or general test tubes
Multiwell plates
Music or message on hold player
Music or sound editing software
Muzzles
Narcotic test kits
Nasal exam specula or dilators
Nasogastric tubes
Nasopharyngeal tubes
Nasopharyngoscopes or accessories
Nebulizers or accessories
Necropsy tables or accessories
Needle guides
Needle or blade or other sharp disposal containers or carts or accessories
Needle protectors
Needleless intraveneous injection syringe sets or injection cannulas
Needleless vial or bag withdrawal cannulas or adapters or decanters
Needlenose pliers
Nephelometers
Nerve retractors
Network analyzers
Network channel or data service units
Network conferencing software
Network connectivity terminal emulation software
Network interface cards
Network monitoring software
Network operating system enhancement software
Network operation system software
Network routers

Network security and virtual private network VPN equipment software
Network security or virtual private network VPN management software
Network switches
Neurological diagnostic sets
Neurological sensors
Neuromuscular stimulators or kits
Nibblers
Night sticks
Nitrogen gas analyzers
Nitrogen or nitrate or nitrite analyzer
Nitroglycerin
Non carbonated beverage dispenser
Non contact sensors
Non invasive bi level machines
Non invasive continuous positive air pressure machines
Non temperature controlled tanker trailers
Non vacuum blood collection tubes or containers
Notebook computers
Nuclear fuel element failure detection systems
Nuclear fuel rod
Nuclear magnetic resonance NMR spectrometers
Nuclear reactor control rod systems
Nuclear reactor earthquake instrumentation
Nuclear tools
Nut drivers
Nut splitters
Nylon rope
Object or component oriented development software

Object oriented data base management software
Odor control equipment
Office suite software
Offset printing plate processors
Offset printing presses
Offset socket wrenches
Ohmmeters
Oil can
Oil content monitors analyzers
Oil filters
Oil gun
Oil pumps
Oilfield production spoolers
Opacity or dust or visibility sensors
Open end wrenches
Open stream current meters
Open stream water level recorders
Operating room lighting for surgical field or accessories or related products
Operating room patient fracture tables or orthopedic tables or accessories or related products
Operating room patient positioning devices or accessories
Operating room patient procedure tables or accessories or related products
Operating system software
Operational amplifiers
Ophthalmic drums or its accessories
Ophthalmic eye test lenses or accessories
Ophthalmic instrument tables or accessories
Ophthalmic irrigation or aspiration supplies or accessories
Ophthalmic lens holders
Ophthalmic lensometers

Ophthalmic medical instrument sets
Ophthalmic perimeters
Ophthalmic prisms
Ophthalmic retinoscope accessories
Ophthalmic retinoscopes
Ophthalmic slit lamps
Ophthalmic surgery instrument sets
Ophthalmic surgical knives or blades or scissors or accessories
Ophthalmic tonometers or accessories
Ophthalmic transilluminators
Ophthalmic visual function analyzers
Ophthalmoscopes or otoscopes or scope sets
Opthalmic retractors
Optical beamsplitters
Optical breadboards
Optical calibration sets
Optical character reader OCR or scanning software
Optical character recognition systems
Optical choppers
Optical diffraction apparatus
Optical diffusers
Optical mounts
Optical network management software
Optical rails or bases
Optical vacuum coating equipment
Opticians tools or accessories
Oral liquid medication syringes
Oral retractors
Orbital shakers
Orbital shaking water baths
Organic carbon analyzers
Organic light emitting displays
Orifice plate

Orthodontic appliance clasps
Orthodontic brackets
Orthodontic ligature cartridges
Orthodontic pliers
Orthodontic setter bands
Orthopedic retractors
Orthopedic splint systems
Orthopedic traction hardware or weights
Orthopedic traction softgoods for general use
Orthotics or foot care products
Oscillographs
Oscilloscopes
Osmometers
Ostomy appliances
Ostomy starter kits
Otological instruments or accessories
Overhead projectors
Oxygen air blenders
Oxygen concentrators
Oxygen delivery connectors or adapters
Oxygen gas analyzers
Oxygen generators
Oxygen insufflator or its accessories
Oxygen monitors or supplies
Oxygen sensors
Oxygen therapy delivery system products accessories or its supplies
Ozone analyzers
Ozone generator
Packaged water treatment systems
Packaging compactors
Packaging vacuum
Page turners for the physically challenged
Pagers
Paging controllers
Paint brushes
Paint mixers

Paint robots
Paint rollers
Paint sprayers
Paint strainers
Paint systems ovens
Paint tester
Pallet trucks
Paper cutting machines or accessories
Paper drilling machines
Paper jogging machines
Paper or pad holder or dispensers
Paper punching or binding machines
Paper shredding machines or accessories
Paper sorting machines
Parachutes
Parallel bars for rehabilitation or therapy
Paramagnetic susceptibility analyzers
Particle size measuring apparatus
Passenger or automobile ferries
Pasteur or transfer pipettes
Patient bed or table scales for general use
Patient carbon dioxide detectors
Patient care beds or accessories for general use
Patient care beds or accessories for specialty care
Patient ceiling hoists
Patient controlled analgesia infusion pumps
Patient floor scales
Patient height rulers
Patient identification products
Patient lifts or accessories
Patient motion sensors or alarms or accessories
Patient scooters

Patient shifting boards or accessories
Patient stabilization or fall prevention devices or accessories
Patient stretchers or stretcher accessories
Pattern design software
Paving breaker tools or accessories
Paving breakers
Paving material mixers
Pawls
PCR enclosures
Peak flowmeters
Pedal exercisers for rehabilitation or therapy
Pediatric or microflow or scalp vein intravenous or arterial catheters
Pedometers
Pelvis or back traction supplies
Penetrometers
Percussion instrument accessory
Perforating machines
Perfusion oxygen or hematocrit saturation monitors or accessories
Perfusion oxygenators or accessories
Pericardiocentesis needles or kits or accessories
Periodontal chisels
Periodontal curettes
Periodontal hoes
Periodontal knives
Periosteotomes
Peripheral controller cards
Peripheral intravenous catheters for general use
Peristaltic pumps
Permeability or porosity estimation apparatus
Permeability testing apparatus
Personal computers

Personal digital assistant PDAs or organizers
Personal motorized watercraft
Pestle or mortars
Petri plates or dishes
pH electrodes
pH meters
pH test strips or papers
Phacoemulsification or extrusion equipment or accessories for ophthalmic surgery
Phantom dosimeters
Pharmaceutical filters or ultra filters
Pharyngeal airways
Pharyngeal airways or airways kits
Phase shifters
Phasemeters
Phlebotomy trays or accessories
Phone headsets
Phoropter units
Photo attachments for microscopes
Photo tubes
Photocopiers
Photoelastic testing instruments
Photoelectric sensors
Photographic enlargers
Photogravure printing machines
Photometers
Photosensitive diodes
Physiological recorders
Pianos
Pick or place robots
Picks
Piezo electric crystals
Pilates machines
Pile drivers
Pipe bending mandrels
Pipe bending tools
Pipe extractors
Pipe handling equipment
Pipe layer

Pipe or tube cutters
Pipe vises
Pipe wrenches
Pipette bulbs
Pipette pumps
Pipette washers
Pipetter inserts or accessories
Pisciculture supplies
Pitch measuring instruments
Pivotal traction therapy supplies
Planes
Planing machines
Plant samples analysis equipment
Planters
Plasma screens
Plasma welding machinery
Plaster or mortar mixers
Plastic injection moldings
Plastic injection molds
Plastic surgery retractors
Plate incubators
Platelet mixers
Platemakers
Platform interconnectivity software
Platform lift
Playing cards
Pleural cavity drainage unit or accessories
Plotter printers
Ploughs
Plumb bobs
Pneumatic actuators
Pneumatic aircraft accumulators
Pneumatic drill
Pneumatic grinders
Pneumatic hammer
Pneumatic impact wrenches
Pneumatic nail drivers
Pneumatic rock drills
Pneumatic sanding machines
Pneumatic vacuum equipment

Pocket watches
Point drivers or accessories for picture frames
Point of sale credit or debit verification kits
Point of sale POS receipt printers
Point of sale POS software
Point of sale POS terminal
Point plotting recorders
Pointers
Polarimeters
Polariscopes
Polarizers
Polarizing microscopes
Police or security shotguns
Police vehicles
Polishing machines
Pollination equipment or supplies
Pool cues
Porosimeters
Portable data input terminals
Portable seismic apparatus
Portable stereo systems
Portal server software
Positioning devices
Positioning jig
Positive displacement pumps
Post hole digger
Postal scales
Postmortem blood detection kits or supplies
Postmortem fingerprint or impression materials
Postmortem incision clips
Postmortem needles
Potentiometers
Potters wheels for hand made ceramics
Powder boards for rehabilitation or therapy
Power blowers
Power buffers
Power buggies
Power caulking guns
Power chippers

Power drills
Power grinders
Power meters
Power nail guns
Power planes
Power routers
Power sanders
Power saws
Power screwguns
Power staple guns
Power supply transformers
Power trimmers
Powered instrument cleaning devices or accessories
Precious metal die castings
Precipitation or evaporation recorders
Premise branch exchange PBX systems
Presentation software
Presses
Pressure controllers
Pressure indicators
Pressure or steam cleaners
Pressure or vacuum recorders
Pressure regulator
Pressure sensors
Pressure stylus
Pressure transmitters
Print servers
Printer driver software
Printing assemblers
Printing collators or decollators
Printing cutters
Printing guillotines
Printing presses
Prisms
Process air heaters
Processing tanks
Procurement software
Profile projectors
Program testing software
Programmable tube furnaces
Progressive cavity pumps

Project management software
Projection screens
Protective aprons
Protective coats
Protective coveralls
Protective gloves
Protective shirts
Protein analyzers
Protocol analyzers
Proton spectrometers
Protractors
Proximity sensors
Pry bars
Psychrometers
Public address systems
Pull spring balances
Pulled scrapers
Pullers
Pulleys or accessories for rehabilitation or therapy
Pulmonary function calculators
Pulmonary functioning tubing or accessories
Pulse oximeter unit accessories
Pulse oximeter units
Pulverizing machinery
Punches or nail sets or drifts
Punching pliers
Pushcarts
Putty knives
Puzzles
Pycnometers
Pyrometers
Q Meters
Radarbased surveillance systems
Radiation detectors
Radio antennas
Radio frequency data communication equipment
Radio frequency identification devices
Radio frequency RF cable
Radio frequency RF switches

Radio frequency scanners
Radio frequency transmitters or receivers
Radio navigation instruments
Radioactive waste disposal systems
Radiobiological effect microdosimeters
Radiographic film or cassette changers
Radiographic locators
Radiometer
Radiosonde apparatus
Radiosurgical gamma knife units or scintillators
Radiotherapy teletherapy cobalt 60 equipment
Radon detectors
Rafts
Rail couplers
Rail switching systems
Railway signaling systems
Rainfall recorders
Rakes
Rangefinders
Rapid amplification or complementary deoxyribonucleic acid ends
RACE technology products
Rasps
Ratchets
Razor knives
Razors
Reachers for the physically challenged
Reactors
Reactors or fermenters or digesters
Read write digital versatile disc DVD
Reagent kits for use with air samplers
Reamers
Receipts or receipt books
Reciprocating compressors
Reciprocating pumps
Reciprocating shaking water baths

Recreational motorboats
Recreational rowboats
Recreational sailboats
Rectal retractors
Rectifiers
Reflectometers
Reflex hammers or mallets
Reforestation equipment
Refrigerant compressors
Refrigerated and heated reach in environmental or growth chambers
Refrigerated and heated walk in environmental or growth chambers
Refrigerated baths
Refrigerated benchtop centrifuges
Refrigerated cooling modules
Refrigerated tanks
Relay boards or multiple relay modules
Remote reading thermometers
Removal devices of diagnostic or interventional vascular catheters or sets
Removal jig
Requirements analysis and system architecture software
Rescue ships or boats
Resectoscopes
Resin guns
Resistance bands
Resistance thermometers
Resistance tubes
Resistive exercise bands or putty or tubing or accessories for rehabilitation or therapy
Resistivity geophysical instruments
Respiration air supplying self contained breathing apparatus or accessories
Respirators

Respiratory aspirator products or accessories
Respiratory humidifiers or vaporizers
Respiratory manometer kits
Respiratory monitoring kits or its accessories
Respiratory therapy compressors
Restraint straps or buckles or accessories or supplies
Restraint vests and jackets
Restraints
Resurfacers
Resuscitation kits
Resuscitation masks or accessories
Retaining ring pliers
Reverse osmosis equipment
Rheometers
Rice cleaning or hulling equipment
Riot batons
Riot helmets
Riot shields
Rivet tools
Road pavers
Road rooters
Road surface heater planers
Road wideners
Roasting machinery
Robot machines
Robotic or automated liquid handling systems
Rock crushers
Rock cutters
Rod pumps
Roll crushers
Roller skates or roller blades
Rollers
Rollers for lawn or sports grounds
Roof rippers
Roofing brushes
Roofing mops
Rope float lines

Rotameters
Rotary drills
Rotary position sensors
Rotary pumps
Rotary tiller mixers
Rotating piston pumps
Rotating shakers
Rough terrain cranes
Roughness measuring instruments
Roulette wheels
Route navigation software
Rowing machines
Rubber or plastic presses
Rulers
S hooks
Saddles
Safety boots
Safety chains
Safety glasses
Safety harnesses or belts
Safety helmets
Safety hoods
Safety hooks
Safety shoes
Safety valves
Salinity meter
Sample changers
Sample holders
Sample oxidizer
Sample preparation bombs
Sampling manifolds
Sampling pumps
Sampling syringes
Sand or water tables or activity centers
Sand testing apparatus
Sanding blocks
Sanding machines
Satellite core equipment
Satellite receivers
Saw blades
Saw guide
Sawing machines
Saws
Scaffolding
Scaffolding stabilizers
Scales
Scanners

Scanning electron microscopes
Scanning light or spinning disk or laser scanning microscopes
Scanning probe microscopes
Scarifiers
Scintillation crystal assemblies
Scissor lift
Scouring pads
Scrapers
Screw extractors
Screw Pumps
Screwdrivers
Scribers
Scrubbing machines
Scuba regulators
Sealant adhesive robots
Secateurs or pruning shears
Security cameras
Security or access control systems
Security tags
Sedimentological analyzing unit
Seed drills
Seed treating equipment
Seeder attachment
Seismic geophones
Seismic receivers
Seismic recorders or seismographs
Semiconductor process systems
Semiconductor testers
Sequential forming machines
Serial port cards
Server load balancer
Sewage pumps
Sewing machines
Sewing needles
Sextants
Sexual assault determination kits
Shaking incubators

Sharpening stones or tools or kits
Shear strength testers
Shears
Sheaves or pulleys
Sheet metal pliers
Shim
Shock testing apparatus
Shoring equipment
Short wave diathermy units
Shot peen machine
Shotcrete spraying equipment
Shovels
Shower or bath chairs or seats for the physically challenged
Shuffleboard
Sifting machinery
Sight flow windows
Signal cable
Signal conditioners
Signal converters
Signal generators
Silencer sections
Silk screen printing machines
Silk screen vacuum printing frames
Silos
Single gas monitors
Skid steer loaders
Skin retractors
Skinfold calipers
Skis
Sleep study monitors or accessories
Slicing machinery
Slickline chemical cutters
Slickline jet cutters
Slickline severing tools
Slide dryers
Slide projectors
Slings
Slip or groove joint pliers
Sloped reading tables
Sludge collectors
Sludge disposal equipment
Sludge or sewage digesters

Sludge or sewage handling trucks
Sludge or sewage removal equipment
Sludge pelletizers
Sludge shredders
Slush machines
Smoke detectors
Smoking machinery
Snow blowers
Snowboards
Snowmobiles or snow scooter
Snowplow attachments
Soap dispensing brush
Socket sets
Sockets
Soft serve machines
Softballs
Soil core sampling apparatus
Soil testing kits
Solar radiation surface observing apparatus
Soldering irons or guns
Soldering or desoldering or combined stations
Solid phase extraction preparations
Solution strength estimation apparatus
Solvent recyclers
Sonars
Sonometers
Sorters
Sorting machines for seed or grain or dried leguminous vegetables
Sound measuring apparatus or decibel meter
Space heaters
Spades
Spanner wrenches
Spatulas
Special hoses
Special purpose telephones
Specialty brushes
Specialty plates for bacteria
Specialty wrenches

Specimen collectors
Specimen holders
Spectrofluorimeters or fluorimeters
Spectrographs
Spectrometers
Spectrophotometers
Speech mirror
Speed sensors
Speed stoppers
Spell checkers
Spherometers
Spill kits
Spinal trays or needles
Spine boards
Spine or neuro retractors
Spiral wrapping
Spirit burners
Spirometers or its accessories or its supplies
Sponges
Sport scoreboards
Sporting traps
Spray booths
Spray dryers
Sprayers
Spreadsheet software
Sputum collection apparatus or containers
Squares
Squeegees or washers
Stackers
Stage or studio lighting systems
Stair climbers
Stamping dies or punches
Stamping or forming dies
Standalone telephone caller identification
Standard fermentation units
Staple guns
Stapler units
Staplers
Staplers for internal use
Staplers for skin closure
Stationary bicycles
Stationary separation equipment or parts or screens

Steam autoclaves or sterilizers
Steam engines
Steam generators
Steam pressing machines
Steaming machinery
Steering wheel puller
Stencils or lettering aids
Stenotype machines
Step aerobic equipment
Step drive or stepper drive or step indexer
Step stool
Stereo or dissecting light microscopes
Sterile or aseptic processing or filling machines
Sterilization biological kits
Sterilization cabinets
Sterilization cleaning brushes
Sterilization heat sealers
Sterilization indicator strips
Sterilization sets
Sterilization test packs and accessories
Sternum retractors
Stethoscopic phonocardiographs
Still cameras
Stirring hotplates
Stomachers
Storage media loading software
Storage networking software
Storage tanks
Straight edges
Strain gauges
Strap wrenches
Strapping dispenser
Strapping tensioners or sealers
Streetcars or tramway cars
Striking hammers
String or twine
Stripping tools
Stroboscopes
Stud finders

Stuffed animals or puppets
Stunner
Subsoilers
Substation load control switchgears
Suction cups
Suction kits
Suction pumps
Suction tube or tubing
Sugar analyzers
Sulfur dioxide analyzers or detectors
Sump pumps
Surface data logging sensors
Surface data logging units
Surface tension measuring instruments
Surface testers
Surface thermometers
Surfboards
Surgeon caps or hoods
Surgical blanket or solution warming cabinets or accessories
Surgical bolt or cable or pin or wire cutter instruments
Surgical bone biopsy mills or related products
Surgical bone biopsy trephines
Surgical bone cutting forceps
Surgical bone hand saws or wire saws or saw handles
Surgical burs or its accessories
Surgical calipers or rulers
Surgical chisels or gouges
Surgical clamps or clips or forceps or accessories
Surgical controller instruments
Surgical curettes or loops
Surgical depressors
Surgical dermatomes or dermabraders or dermameshers or accessories

Surgical dilators or accessories
Surgical dissectors
Surgical drains or sets or accessories
Surgical drapes
Surgical drivers or its parts or accessories
Surgical elevators or levers
Surgical equipment stands or accessories
Surgical extractors
Surgical gloves
Surgical hammers or mallets
Surgical hand or twist drills or drill kits or accessories
Surgical impactors or packers
Surgical instrument holders or positioners
Surgical irrigation or suction handpieces or cannulas or cystotomes or tips or related products
Surgical irrigation sets or accessories
Surgical isolation suits or helmets or facemasks or accessories
Surgical lasers or accessories
Surgical lighted fiberoptic retractors
Surgical lithotripters or accessories
Surgical manipulating instruments
Surgical microscopes or loops or magnifiers or accessories
Surgical mouth gags or accessories
Surgical needle holders for general use
Surgical nerve stimulators or accessories
Surgical nippers

Surgical or endoscopic catheters or catheterization kits or drainage bags
Surgical perfusion catheters or connectors or accessories
Surgical pliers
Surgical pneumatic or battery or electric saws or drills or pin drivers or accessories
Surgical pneumatic or electric tourniquets or accessories
Surgical power equipment sets or accessories
Surgical probes or directors
Surgical punches or punch holder or accessories
Surgical purstring devices
Surgical rake retractors
Surgical rasps
Surgical retraction hooks
Surgical retractors for general use
Surgical ronguers
Surgical scalpels or knives or blades or trephines or accessories
Surgical scissors
Surgical shave kits or prep razors or clippers
Surgical smoke evacuators or accessories
Surgical sounds
Surgical spatulas
Surgical specula
Surgical spreaders
Surgical sterile instrument brushes or instrument stylets or instrument wipes
Surgical suction machines or vacuum extractors or ultrasonic surgical aspirators or regulators or accessories
Surgical suction or irrigation tubings or accessories

Surgical suture or wire passers or related products
Surgical taps
Surgical tomes
Surgical tourniquets or vascular occluders or ligators or accessories
Surgical tracheal stents
Surgical trocars for general use or accessories
Surgical urology retractors or its accessories
Surgical vacuum extraction devices or curettes or related products
Surveillance video or audio recorders
Suture needles
Suture removal kits or trays or packs or sets
Suture removers
Suturing kits or trays or packs or sets
Swab collection or transport containers
Swaging tools
Swim goggles or swim fins
Switch or router software
Switchyard disconnect switches
Swivel hooks
Syringe pumps
T handle tap wrenches
T squares
Table gambling management systems
Table tennis paddles
Tablet computers
Tablet counters
Tablet crushers or accessories
Tachometers
Tactile toys
Tampers
Tangent benders
Tankers
Tap extractors
Tap machines or tapping machines

Tape arrays
Tape drive libraries
Tape drives
Tape measures
Taps or dies
Tarpaulins
Tax preparation software
Teeth cleaning devices or accessories
Telecommunication devices TDD or teletypewriters TTY for the physically challenged
Teleconference equipment
Telegraph sounders
Telephony equipment service observing units
Telescopes
Telescoping boom lift
Teletype input devices
Televisions
Temperature calibrator or simulator
Temperature controlled container trailers
Temperature cycling chambers or thermal cyclers
Temperature humidity testers
Temperature indicating sticks
Temperature or humidity surface observing apparatus
Temperature regulators
Temperature transmitters
Templates
Tennis racquets
Tensiometers
Tension testers
Tensioners
Terminations
Test sieves
Test tube racks
Theodolites
Therapeutic balls or accessories
Therapeutic cryo compression therapy systems

Therapeutic heating or cooling blankets or drapes
Therapeutic heating or cooling pads or compresses or packs
Therapeutic heating or cooling units or systems
Therapeutic ice packs or pillows
Therapeutic paraffin baths or accessories
Therapeutic pegboards or activity boards
Thermal book binding machines
Thermal conductivity analyzers
Thermal differential analyzers
Thermal engines
Thermal tape printers
Thermistors
Thermo gravimetry analyzers
Thermocouple probes
Thermocouples
Thermographs
Thermometer probes
Thermostats
Thickness measuring devices
Thin client computers
Thin layer chromatography tanks
Thinlayer chromatographs
Thoracentesis sets or trays
Thread counters or gauges
Threading dies
Threading machines
Threading taps
Threshing machines
Through tubing perforation guns
Ticket dispensing machines
Tie down anchors
Tilt trucks
Time accounting software
Tinners snips
Tire changing machines

Tissue culture apparatus
Tissue culture coated plates or dishes or inserts
Tissue culture flasks
Tissue culture incubators
Tissue embedding stations
Tissue flotation baths
Tissue processors
Tissue retractors
Titration equipment
Toilet brushes
Tongs
Tongue and groove pliers
Tongue depressors or blades or sticks
Tool template sets
Torque converters
Torque tools
Torque wrenches
Torsion testers
Torso and belt restraints
Torx keys
Touch pads
Touch screen monitors
Touring bicycles
Tourniquets
Tow trucks
Tower cranes
Toxicology analyzers
Toxicology test kits or supplies
Tracheal retractors
Tracheostomy accessories
Tracheostomy tubes
Track bulldozers
Track cranes
Track excavators
Track loaders
Traction splint sets
Traffic signals
Trailer hitches
Train braking systems
Train defrosting or defogging systems
Training ramps for rehabilitation or therapy
Training stairs for rehabilitation or therapy

Transaction security and virus protection software
Transaction server software
Transcutaneous electric nerve stimulation units
Transilluminators
Transistor circuit testers
Transistor transistor logic TTL
Transmission electron microscopes
Transplanters
Transport or mobile multiparameter vital sign units or accessories
Transport ventilators
Trapshooting equipment
Trash bags
Treadmill exercisers for rehabilitation or therapy
Treadmills
Trenching machines
Triangles
Trim or molding tools
Triple beam balances
Trowels
Truck or rail scales
Tube bending machinery
Tube end finishers
Tube furnaces
Tube rotators
Tuberculin syringes
Tug boats
Tumblers or polishers
Tungsten carbide abrasive wheels
Tungsten inert gas TIG welding machinery
Turbidimeters
Turbine engines
Turbine pumps
Turnbuckles
Turning machines
Turntables
Tweezers
Twin screw extruder
Twist drills
Two way radios

Tympanometers or accessories
Typewriters
Ultra cold or ultralow upright cabinets or freezers
Ultra pure water systems
Ultra violet water purification units
Ultracentrifuges
Ultrafiltration equipment
Ultrasonic cleaning equipment
Ultrasonic disintegrators
Ultrasonic examination equipment
Ultrasonic therapy apparatus or supplies
Ultrasound welding machinery
Ultraviolet crosslinkers
Ultraviolet disinfection equipment
Ultraviolet UV lamps
Umbilical catheters
Underwater cameras
Upper body resistance machines
Upper extremity prosthetic devices
Urinalysis analyzers
Urinalysis test strips
Urinary catheterization kits or accessories
Urological procedure trays or packs or kits
Urological surgical instrument sets
Uterine devices or accessories
Uterine retractors
Utility knives
Vacuum blood collection tubes or containers
Vacuum cleaner supplies or accessories
Vacuum cleaners
Vacuum desiccators
Vacuum gauges
Vacuum molding machines

Vacuum or centrifugal concentrators
Vacuum or mercury vapour equipment
Vacuum or rotary evaporators
Vacuum ovens
Vacuum pumps
Vacuum tube needles
Vaginal exam specula
Vaginal ultrasound or echo probes or accessories
Valve actuators
Variable resistors or varistors
Vascular imaging guidewires or snares or accessories
Vascular or compression apparel or supports
Vascular sequential compression devices or tubing
Vehicle horns
Vehicle navigation systems
Vehicle traction control systems
Vehicular global positioning systems
Vein harvest systems
Vein retractors
Ventilator accessories
Ventricular assist devices
Venturis
Vestibular motion devices for rehabilitation or therapy
Veterinary blood pressure testers
Veterinary castration instruments
Veterinary clinical thermometers
Veterinary electrocardiograph ECG
Veterinary injection or suction units or accessories
Veterinary nail trimmers or cutters
Veterinary speculums

Vibration testers
Vibratory plates
Vibratory separation equipment or parts or screens
Video attachments for microscopes
Video cassette players or recorders
Video conference cameras
Video conferencing software
Video creation and editing software
Video editors
Video monitors
Video streaming system
Videoconferencing systems
Videoscopes
Viscosimeters
Vision testing stereoscopes
Visual filters
Visual presenters
Voice mail systems
Voice recognition software
Voice synthesizers for the physically challenged
Volleyballs
Voltage comparator integrated circuits
Voltage or current meters
Volumeters
Volumetric pipettes
Vortex mixers
Vulcanizing machines
Wagons
Walkers or rollators
Walking braces
Wallpaper roller
WAN switching software and firmware
Warming cabinets
Water analysis systems
Water analyzers
Water based paints
Water baths
Water conditioners
Water filters
Water hoses

Water jacketed single chamber three gas incubators
Water meters
Water pumps
Water purification equipment
Water samplers
Water skis or accessories
Water softening accessories
Water sprinklers
Water treatment dryers
Water trucks
Water tube boiler
Wattmeters
Wave generators
Weapons or explosives detectors
Wear testers
Wearable computing devices
Weather stations
Weaving accessories
Web page creation and editing software
Web platform development software
Wedges
Weeders
Weight machines for rehabilitation or therapy
Weight measuring instrument accessories
Weights or accessories for rehabilitation or therapy
Welders
Welding electrodes
Welding generators
Welding masks
Welding or brazing tip cleaner files
Welding or cutting tips
Welding or soldering kit
Welding robots
Welding tip dressers or accessories
Welding tools
Welding wire

Well logging downhole test equipment
Well testing downhole tools
Wellhead beam pumps
Wet mops
Wet or dry combination vacuum cleaners
Wet scrubbers
Wetsuits
Wheel alignment equipment
Wheel balancing equipment
Wheel bulldozers
Wheel chocks
Wheel excavators
Wheel loaders
Wheelbarrows
Wheelchair accessories
Wheelchair ramps
Wheelchairs
Winches
Wind surface observing apparatus
Wing benders
Wire brushes
Wire cathode electrode discharge machine
Wire cutters
Wire lug crimping tool
Wire or cable cutters
Wireless software
Wireline grabs
WLAN wireless access network equipment and components
Wood burning tools
Wood chisels
Word processing software
Word processors
Work tables or stations or accessories for rehabilitation or therapy
Workshop cranes
Workshop presses
Wrapping machinery
Wrist exercisers for rehabilitation or therapy
Writing aids for the physically challenged

X ray and fluoroscopy RF radiotherapy planning simulators
X ray bone densitometers
X ray diffraction equipment
X ray generators
X ray radiography examination equipment

Abilities

Together these four clusters, or groupings, are broken down into 52 elements, types or categories, of the major clusters. These are all in the Workbook, in a table so that you can keep track of your abilities. By Ability cluster then, they are:

In the workbook, you will find an exercise that lists the categories within the four major Abilities Clusters. Before you turn to the exercises, why not go to the O*NET website and investigate each category, looking for jobs where the item is important. This will help to give you a better "feel" for what each item is.

These are Ability Clusters and the categories within each as listed by the Department of Labor, O*NET website. In the second column rate yourself on each item, on a scale of 1 to 5, where 1 is "not really, 3 is "yeah I've got that", and 5 is "outstanding, top-notch, I really have that skill down." Or something like those informal standards. If you are not sure, go the the website and poke around awhile. Look for jobs in each category and then at jobs in the levels of those categories. Might as well take the time to figure yourself out. There is no right or wrong but it would make sense to try get and a good handle on your Abilities as they relate to jobs and careers. Wouldn't it? Use the third column to indicate if you like using that particular ability, a simple "Y" for "Yes" and "N" for "No" works fine.

	Rating (1-5)	Like Using It (Y/N)
Cognitive:		
Category Flexibility — The ability to generate or use different sets of rules for combining or grouping things in different ways.		
Deductive Reasoning — The ability to apply general rules to specific problems to produce answers that make sense.		
Flexibility of Closure — The ability to identify or detect a known pattern (a figure, object, word, or sound) that is hidden in other distracting material.		
Fluency of Ideas — The ability to come up with a number of ideas about a topic (the number of ideas is important, not their quality, correctness, or creativity).		
Inductive Reasoning — The ability to combine pieces of information to form general rules or conclusions (includes finding a relationship among seemingly unrelated events).		
Information Ordering — The ability to arrange things or actions in a certain order or pattern according to a specific rule or set of rules (e.g., patterns of numbers, letters, words, pictures, mathematical operations).		

	Rating (1-5)	Like Using It (Y/N)
Mathematical Reasoning — The ability to choose the right mathematical methods or formulas to solve a problem.		
Memorization — The ability to remember information such as words, numbers, pictures, and procedures.		
Number Facility — The ability to add, subtract, multiply, or divide quickly and correctly.		
Oral Comprehension — The ability to listen to and understand information and ideas presented through spoken words and sentences.		
Oral Expression — The ability to communicate information and ideas in speaking so others will understand.		
Originality — The ability to come up with unusual or clever ideas about a given topic or situation, or to develop creative ways to solve a problem.		
Perceptual Speed — The ability to quickly and accurately compare similarities and differences among sets of letters, numbers, objects, pictures, or patterns. The things to be compared may be presented at the same time or one after the other. This ability also includes comparing a presented object with a remembered object.		
Problem Sensitivity — The ability to tell when something is wrong or is likely to go wrong. It does not involve solving the problem, only recognizing there is a problem.		
Selective Attention — The ability to concentrate on a task over a period of time without being distracted.		
Spatial Orientation — The ability to know your location in relation to the environment or to know where other objects are in relation to you.		
Speed of Closure — The ability to quickly make sense of, combine, and organize information into meaningful patterns.		
Time Sharing — The ability to shift back and forth between two or more activities or sources of information (such as speech, sounds, touch, or other sources).		

	Rating (1-5)	Like Using It (Y/N)
Visualization — The ability to imagine how something will look after it is moved around or when its parts are moved or rearranged.		
Written Comprehension — The ability to read and understand information and ideas presented in writing.		
Written Expression — The ability to communicate information and ideas in writing so others will understand.		
Physical:		
Dynamic Flexibility — The ability to quickly and repeatedly bend, stretch, twist, or reach out with your body, arms, and/or legs.		
Dynamic Strength — The ability to exert muscle force repeatedly or continuously over time. This involves muscular endurance and resistance to muscle fatigue.		
Explosive Strength — The ability to use short bursts of muscle force to propel oneself (as in jumping or sprinting), or to throw an object.		
Extent Flexibility — The ability to bend, stretch, twist, or reach with your body, arms, and/or legs.		
Gross Body Coordination — The ability to coordinate the movement of your arms, legs, and torso together when the whole body is in motion.		
Gross Body Equilibrium — The ability to keep or regain your body balance or stay upright when in an unstable position.		
Stamina — The ability to exert yourself physically over long periods of time without getting winded or out of breath.		
Static Strength — The ability to exert maximum muscle force to lift, push, pull, or carry objects.		
Trunk Strength — The ability to use your abdominal and lower back muscles to support part of the body repeatedly or continuously over time without 'giving out' or fatiguing.		

	Rating (1-5)	Like Using It (Y/N)
Psychomotor:		
Arm-Hand Steadiness — The ability to keep your hand and arm steady while moving your arm or while holding your arm and hand in one position.		
Control Precision — The ability to quickly and repeatedly adjust the controls of a machine or a vehicle to exact positions.		
Finger Dexterity — The ability to make precisely coordinated movements of the fingers of one or both hands to grasp, manipulate, or assemble very small objects.		
Manual Dexterity — The ability to quickly move your hand, your hand together with your arm, or your two hands to grasp, manipulate, or assemble objects.		
Multilimb Coordination — The ability to coordinate two or more limbs (for example, two arms, two legs, or one leg and one arm) while sitting, standing, or lying down. It does not involve performing the activities while the whole body is in motion.		
Rate Control — The ability to time your movements or the movement of a piece of equipment in anticipation of changes in the speed and/or direction of a moving object or scene.		
Reaction Time — The ability to quickly respond (with the hand, finger, or foot) to a signal (sound, light, picture) when it appears.		
Response Orientation — The ability to choose quickly between two or more movements in response to two or more different signals (lights, sounds, pictures). It includes the speed with which the correct response is started with the hand, foot, or other body part.		
Speed of Limb Movement — The ability to quickly move the arms and legs.		
Wrist-Finger Speed — The ability to make fast, simple, repeated movements of the fingers, hands, and wrists.		
Sensory:		

	Rating (1-5)	Like Using It (Y/N)
Auditory Attention — The ability to focus on a single source of sound in the presence of other distracting sounds.		
Depth Perception — The ability to judge which of several objects is closer or farther away from you, or to judge the distance between you and an object.		
Far Vision — The ability to see details at a distance.		
Glare Sensitivity — The ability to see objects in the presence of glare or bright lighting.		
Hearing Sensitivity — The ability to detect or tell the differences between sounds that vary in pitch and loudness.		
Near Vision — The ability to see details at close range (within a few feet of the observer).		
Night Vision — The ability to see under low light conditions.		
Peripheral Vision — The ability to see objects or movement of objects to one's side when the eyes are looking ahead.		
Sound Localization — The ability to tell the direction from which a sound originated.		
Speech Clarity — The ability to speak clearly so others can understand you.		
Speech Recognition — The ability to identify and understand the speech of another person.		
Visual Color Discrimination — The ability to match or detect differences between colors, including shades of color and brightness.		

Work Activities

None of this is section is referenced in the "It's Your Future" book, it is all Bonus Material.

We are going to present three tables of Work Activity Information for you to use to consider what you like or might like to do. They are arranged from the shortest (42 choices) to the longest (2,070 choices). These also go from the broadest categories to the narrowest. Are they definitive? Could there be more? Sure but this is as good a starting point as you are likely to stumble upon.

Work Activity

Analyzing Data or Information
Assisting and Caring for Others
Coaching and Developing Others
Communicating with Persons Outside Organization
Communicating with Supervisors, Peers, or Subordinates
Controlling Machines and Processes
Coordinating the Work and Activities of Others
Developing and Building Teams
Developing Objectives and Strategies
Documenting/Recording Information
Drafting, Laying Out, and Specifying Technical Devices, Parts, and Equipment
Establishing and Maintaining Interpersonal Relationships
Estimating the Quantifiable Characteristics of Products, Events, or Information
Evaluating Information to Determine Compliance with Standards
Getting Information
Guiding, Directing, and Motivating Subordinates
Handling and Moving Objects
Identifying Objects, Actions, and Events
Inspecting Equipment, Structures, or Material
Interacting With Computers
Interpreting the Meaning of Information for Others
Judging the Qualities of Things, Services, or People
Making Decisions and Solving Problems
Monitor Processes, Materials, or Surroundings
Monitoring and Controlling Resources
Operating Vehicles, Mechanized Devices, or Equipment
Organizing, Planning, and Prioritizing Work
Performing Administrative Activities
Performing for or Working Directly with the Public
Performing General Physical Activities
Processing Information
Provide Consultation and Advice to Others
Repairing and Maintaining Electronic Equipment
Repairing and Maintaining Mechanical Equipment
Resolving Conflicts and Negotiating with Others
Scheduling Work and Activities
Selling or Influencing Others
Staffing Organizational Units
Thinking Creatively
Training and Teaching Others
Updating and Using Relevant Knowledge

The second and longer table.

Work Activity

Adjust equipment to ensure adequate performance.
Adjust medical equipment to ensure adequate performance.
Administer basic health care or medical treatments.
Administer diagnostic tests to assess patient health.
Administer emergency medical treatment.
Administer therapeutic treatments.
Advise others on business or operational matters.
Advise others on educational or vocational matters.
Advise others on environmental sustainability or green practices.
Advise others on financial matters.
Advise others on healthcare or wellness issues.
Advise others on legal or regulatory matters.
Advise others on products or services.
Advise others on the design or use of technologies.
Advise others on workplace health or safety issues.
Advise patients or clients on medical issues.
Advocate for individual or community needs.
Alter audio or video recordings.
Analyze biological or chemical substances or related data.
Analyze business or financial data.
Analyze business or financial risks.
Analyze data to improve operations.
Analyze environmental or geospatial data.
Analyze health or medical data.
Analyze market or industry conditions.
Analyze performance of systems or equipment.
Analyze scientific or applied data using mathematical principles.
Apply decorative finishes.
Apply hygienic or cosmetic agents to skin or hair.
Apply materials to fill gaps or imperfections.
Apply protective solutions or coatings.
Arrange displays or decorations.
Assemble equipment or components.
Assemble products or work aids.
Assess characteristics of land or property.
Assess characteristics or impacts of regulations or policies.
Assess compliance with environmental standards or regulations.
Assess living, work, or social needs or status of individuals or communities.
Assess student capabilities, needs, or performance.
Assign work to others.
Assist healthcare practitioners during medical procedures.
Assist individuals with paperwork.
Assist individuals with special needs.
Assist others to access additional services or resources.
Assist scientists, scholars, or technical specialists with projects or research.
Authorize business activities or transactions.
Build structures.
Calculate financial data.
Care for plants or animals.
Clean medical equipment or facilities.
Clean tools, equipment, facilities, or work areas.
Clean workpieces, finished products, or other objects.
Climb equipment or structures.
Coach others.
Collaborate in the development of educational programs.
Collect data about consumer needs or opinions.
Collect environmental or biological samples.

Collect fares or payments.
Collect information about patients or clients.
Collect samples of products or materials.
Communicate environmental or sustainability information.
Communicate with others about business strategies.
Communicate with others about operational plans or activities.
Communicate with others about specifications or project details.
Compile records, documentation, or other data.
Conduct amusement or gaming activities.
Confer with clients to determine needs or order specifications.
Confer with healthcare or other professionals about patient care.
Connect components or supply lines to equipment or tools.
Consult legal materials or public records.
Coordinate activities with clients, agencies, or organizations.
Coordinate artistic or entertainment activities.
Coordinate group, community, or public activities.
Coordinate regulatory compliance activities.
Coordinate with others to resolve problems.
Counsel others about personal matters.
Create artistic designs or performances.
Create decorative objects or parts of objects.
Create visual designs or displays.
Cut materials.
Cut trees or other vegetation.
Design computer or information systems or applications.
Design databases.
Design electrical or electronic systems or equipment.
Design industrial systems or equipment.
Design materials or devices.
Design structures or facilities.
Determine operational methods or procedures.
Determine resource needs of projects or operations.
Determine values or prices of goods or services.
Develop business or marketing plans.
Develop contingency or emergency response plans.
Develop educational programs, plans, or procedures.
Develop financial or business plans.
Develop health assessment methods or programs.
Develop marketing or promotional materials.
Develop models of systems, processes, or products.
Develop news, entertainment, or artistic content.
Develop operational or technical procedures or standards.
Develop organizational or program goals or objectives.
Develop organizational policies, systems, or processes.
Develop patient or client care or treatment plans.
Develop plans for managing or preserving natural resources.
Develop professional relationships or networks.
Develop public or community health programs.
Develop recipes or menus.
Develop research plans or methodologies.
Develop safety standards, policies, or procedures.
Develop scientific or mathematical theories or models.
Develop sustainable organizational or business policies or practices.
Develop systems or practices to mitigate or resolve environmental problems.
Develop technical specifications for products or operations.
Diagnose health conditions or disorders.
Diagnose system or equipment problems.
Direct construction or extraction activities.
Direct legal activities.
Direct organizational operations, activities, or procedures.
Direct scientific or technical activities.
Direct security or safety activities or operations.

Direct vehicle traffic.
Disassemble equipment.
Discuss legal matters with clients, disputants, or legal professionals or staff.
Dispose of waste or debris.
Distribute materials, supplies, or resources.
Document technical designs, procedures, or activities.
Draft legislation or regulations.
Drill holes in earth or materials.
Edit written materials or documents.
Embalm corpses.
Engrave objects.
Escort others.
Estimate project development or operational costs.
Evaluate condition of financial assets, property, or other resources.
Evaluate designs, specifications, or other technical data.
Evaluate green technologies or processes.
Evaluate patient or client condition or treatment options.
Evaluate personnel capabilities or performance.
Evaluate production inputs or outputs.
Evaluate programs, practices, or processes.
Evaluate project feasibility.
Evaluate scholarly work.
Evaluate the characteristics, usefulness, or performance of products or technologies.
Evaluate the quality or accuracy of data.
Examine financial activities, operations, or systems.
Examine materials or documentation for accuracy or compliance.
Examine people or animals to assess health conditions or physical characteristics.
Execute financial transactions.
Explain financial information.
Explain medical information to patients or family members.
Explain regulations, policies, or procedures.
Explain technical details of products or services.
Fabricate devices or components.
Fabricate medical devices.
Fit assistive devices to patients or clients.
Follow standard healthcare safety procedures to protect patient and staff members.
Gather data about operational or development activities.
Gather information for news stories.
Gather information from physical or electronic sources.
Groom or style hair.
Hunt animals.
Identify business or organizational opportunities.
Implement procedures or processes.
Implement security measures for computer or information systems.
Inspect characteristics or conditions of materials or products.
Inspect commercial, industrial, or production systems or equipment.
Inspect completed work or finished products.
Inspect facilities or equipment.
Inspect vehicles.
Install commercial or production equipment.
Install energy or heating equipment.
Install plumbing or piping equipment or systems.
Interpret language, cultural, or religious information for others.
Intervene in crisis situations or emergencies.
Interview people to obtain information.
Investigate criminal or legal matters.
Investigate incidents or accidents.
Investigate individuals' background, behavior, or activities.
Investigate organizational or operational problems.

Investigate the environmental impact of industrial or development activities.
Issue documentation.
Join parts using soldering, welding, or brazing techniques.
Load products, materials, or equipment for transportation or further processing.
Maintain current knowledge in area of expertise.
Maintain electronic, computer, or other technical equipment.
Maintain facilities or equipment.
Maintain health or medical records.
Maintain medical equipment or instruments.
Maintain operational records.
Maintain safety or security.
Maintain sales or financial records.
Maintain tools or equipment.
Maintain vehicles in working condition.
Make legal decisions.
Manage agricultural or forestry operations.
Manage budgets or finances.
Manage control systems or activities.
Manage human resources activities.
Mark materials or objects for identification.
Measure physical characteristics of materials, products, or equipment.
Mediate disputes.
Monitor environmental conditions.
Monitor equipment operation.
Monitor external affairs, trends, or events.
Monitor financial data or activities.
Monitor health conditions of humans or animals.
Monitor individual behavior or performance.
Monitor operation of computer or information technologies.
Monitor operations to ensure adequate performance.
Monitor operations to ensure compliance with regulations or standards.
Monitor resources or inventories.
Monitor safety or security of work areas, facilities, or properties.
Monitor traffic conditions.
Move materials, equipment, or supplies.
Negotiate contracts or agreements.
Notify others of emergencies or problems.
Obtain formal documentation or authorization.
Obtain information about goods or services.
Operate agricultural or forestry equipment.
Operate audiovisual or related equipment.
Operate communications equipment or systems.
Operate computer systems or computerized equipment.
Operate construction or excavation equipment.
Operate cutting or grinding equipment.
Operate energy production or distribution equipment.
Operate industrial processing or production equipment.
Operate laboratory or field equipment.
Operate lifting or moving equipment.
Operate medical equipment.
Operate office equipment.
Operate pumping systems or equipment.
Operate transportation equipment or vehicles.
Order medical tests or procedures.
Package objects.
Perform administrative or clerical activities.
Perform agricultural activities.
Perform athletic activities for fitness, competition, or artistic purposes.
Perform court-related or other legal administrative activities.
Perform general construction or extraction activities.
Perform human resources activities.
Perform recruiting or hiring activities.

Plan events or programs.
Plan work activities.
Position materials or components for assembly.
Position tools or equipment.
Position workpieces or materials on equipment.
Prepare documentation for contracts, applications, or permits.
Prepare financial documents, reports, or budgets.
Prepare foods or beverages.
Prepare health or medical documents.
Prepare industrial materials for processing or use.
Prepare informational or instructional materials.
Prepare legal or regulatory documents.
Prepare medical equipment or work areas for use.
Prepare mixtures or solutions.
Prepare proposals or grant applications.
Prepare reports of operational or procedural activities.
Prepare schedules for services or facilities.
Prepare specimens or materials for testing.
Prescribe medical treatments or devices.
Present arts or entertainment performances.
Present information in legal proceedings.
Present research or technical information.
Process animal carcasses.
Process digital or online data.
Process forensic or legal evidence.
Process shipments or mail.
Program computer systems or production equipment.
Promote products, services, or programs.
Protect people or property from threats such as fires or flooding.
Provide food or beverage services.
Provide general assistance to others, such as customers, patrons, or motorists.
Provide information or assistance to the public.
Provide information to guests, clients, or customers.
Provide support or encouragement to others.
Purchase goods or services.
Read documents or materials to inform work processes.
Reconcile financial data.
Record images with photographic or audiovisual equipment.
Record information about environmental conditions.
Record information about legal matters.
Remove workpieces from production equipment.
Repair electrical or electronic equipment.
Repair tools or equipment.
Repair vehicle components.
Repair workpieces or products.
Replenish inventories of materials, equipment, or products.
Research agricultural processes or practices.
Research biological or ecological phenomena.
Research healthcare issues.
Research historical or social issues.
Research issues related to earth sciences.
Research laws, precedents, or other legal data.
Research organizational behavior, processes, or performance.
Research technology designs or applications.
Resolve computer problems.
Resolve personnel or operational problems.
Respond to customer problems or inquiries.
Schedule appointments.
Schedule operational activities.
Select materials or equipment for operations or projects.
Sell products or services.
Serve on organizational committees.
Set up classrooms, facilities, educational materials, or equipment.
Set up computer systems, networks, or other information systems.

Set up equipment.
Set up protective structures or coverings near work areas.
Sew garments or materials.
Shape materials to create products.
Signal others to coordinate work activities.
Smooth surfaces of objects or equipment.
Sort materials or products.
Stock supplies or products.
Study details of artistic productions.
Supervise activities in correctional facilities.
Supervise personnel activities.
Take physical measurements of patients or clients.
Teach academic or vocational subjects.
Teach life skills.
Teach safety procedures or standards to others.
Tend watercraft.
Test characteristics of materials or products.
Test performance of computer or information systems.
Test performance of equipment or systems.
Test sites or materials for environmental hazards.
Train animals.
Train others on health or medical topics.
Train others on operational or work procedures.
Train others to use equipment or products.
Transport patients or clients.
Treat injuries, illnesses, or diseases.
Verify personal information.
Write material for artistic or commercial purposes.

The third and longest table.

Work Activity
Accompany individuals or groups to activities.
Accompany patients or clients on outings to provide assistance.
Acquire supplies or equipment.
Add garnishes to food.
Adjust dental devices or appliances to ensure fit.
Adjust equipment controls to regulate coolant flow.
Adjust equipment controls to regulate flow of production materials or products.
Adjust equipment controls to regulate flow of water, cleaning solutions, or other liquids.
Adjust equipment controls to regulate gas flow.
Adjust equipment to ensure optimal performance.
Adjust fabrics or other materials during garment production.
Adjust flow of electricity to tools or production equipment.
Adjust office equipment to ensure proper operation.
Adjust position of molds during processing.
Adjust positions of patients on beds or tables.
Adjust prostheses or other assistive devices.
Adjust routes or speeds as necessary.
Adjust settings or positions of medical equipment.
Adjust temperature controls of ovens or other heating equipment.
Adjust the tension of nuts or bolts.
Adjust tuning or functioning of musical instruments.
Adjust vehicle components according to specifications.
Administer anesthetics or sedatives to control pain.
Administer basic health care or medical treatments.
Administer blood or other fluids intravenously.
Administer cancer treatments.
Administer compensation or benefits programs.
Administer drug screening tests.
Administer first aid.
Administer intravenous medications.
Administer medical substances for imaging or other procedures.
Administer non-intravenous medications.
Administer oaths to court participants.
Administer personnel recruitment or hiring activities.
Administer screening tests to determine abilities or treatment needs.
Administer standardized physical or psychological tests.
Administer tests to assess educational needs or progress.
Administer therapeutic massages.
Administer therapy treatments to patients using hands or physical treatment aids.
Advise athletes, coaches, or trainers on exercise regimens, nutrition, or equipment use.
Advise clients or community groups on health issues.
Advise communities or institutions regarding health or safety issues.
Advise customers on technical or procedural issues.
Advise customers on the use of products or services.
Advise educators on curricula, instructional methods, or policies.
Advise medical personnel regarding healthcare issues.
Advise others about environmental management or conservation.
Advise others about land management or conservation.
Advise others on analytical techniques.
Advise others on business or operational matters.
Advise others on career or personal development.
Advise others on educational matters.

Advise others on farming or forestry operations, regulations, or equipment.
Advise others on financial matters.
Advise others on green energy or related technologies.
Advise others on health and safety issues.
Advise others on healthcare matters.
Advise others on human resources topics.
Advise others on issues related to repairs, installation, or equipment design.
Advise others on legal or regulatory compliance matters.
Advise others on logistics topics.
Advise others on management of emergencies or hazardous situations or materials.
Advise others on matters of public policy.
Advise others on social or educational issues.
Advise others on the development or use of new technologies.
Advise others on ways to improve processes or products.
Advise others regarding green practices or environmental concerns.
Advise patients on effects of health conditions or treatments.
Advise patients on healthcare system processes.
Advise patients on preventive care techniques.
Advise real estate clients.
Advise students on academic or career matters.
Advocate for individual or community needs.
Align equipment or machinery.
Align masonry materials.
Align parts or workpieces to ensure proper assembly.
Allocate physical resources within organizations.
Analyze biological samples.
Analyze budgetary or accounting data.
Analyze business or financial data.
Analyze chemical compounds or substances.
Analyze consumer trends.
Analyze costs and benefits of proposed designs or projects.
Analyze crime scene evidence.
Analyze data to assess operational or project effectiveness.
Analyze data to determine project feasibility.
Analyze data to identify or resolve operational problems.
Analyze data to identify trends or relationships among variables.
Analyze data to inform operational decisions or activities.
Analyze data to inform personnel decisions.
Analyze design or requirements information for mechanical equipment or systems.
Analyze design requirements for computer or electronics systems.
Analyze energy usage data.
Analyze environmental data.
Analyze environmental regulations to ensure organizational compliance.
Analyze financial information.
Analyze financial records or reports to determine state of operations.
Analyze financial records to improve budgeting or planning.
Analyze financial records to improve efficiency.
Analyze forecasting data to improve business decisions.
Analyze forensic evidence to solve crimes.
Analyze Geographic Information Systems (GIS) data for use in green applications.
Analyze geological or geographical data.
Analyze geological samples.
Analyze green technology design requirements.
Analyze health-related data.
Analyze impact of legal or regulatory changes.
Analyze industry trends.
Analyze information obtained from news sources.

Analyze jobs using observation, survey, or interview techniques.
Analyze laboratory findings.
Analyze laboratory specimens to detect abnormalities or other problems.
Analyze logistics processes.
Analyze market conditions or trends.
Analyze market or customer related data.
Analyze market research data.
Analyze medical data to determine cause of death.
Analyze operational data to evaluate operations, processes or products.
Analyze operational or research data.
Analyze patient data to determine patient needs or treatment goals.
Analyze physical, survey, or geographic data.
Analyze project data to determine specifications or requirements.
Analyze quantitative data to determine effectiveness of treatments or therapies.
Analyze risks related to investments in green technology.
Analyze risks to minimize losses or damages.
Analyze security of systems, network, or data.
Analyze shipping information to make routing decisions.
Analyze test data or images to inform diagnosis or treatment.
Analyze test or performance data to assess equipment operation.
Analyze test or validation data.
Analyze test results.
Analyze traffic data.
Analyze website or related online data to track trends or usage.
Answer customer questions about goods or services.
Answer telephones to direct calls or provide information.
Apply adhesives to construction materials.
Apply bandages, dressings, or splints.
Apply chemical solutions to plants to protect against disease or insects or to enhance growth.
Apply cleansing or conditioning agents to client hair, scalp, or skin.
Apply decorative coloring to photographs or printed materials.
Apply decorative masonry finishes.
Apply decorative or textured finishes or coverings.
Apply finishes to artwork, crafts, or displays.
Apply identification labels or tags.
Apply information technology to solve business or other applied problems.
Apply knowledge or research findings to address environmental problems.
Apply lubricants or coolants to workpieces.
Apply makeup to alter or enhance appearance.
Apply material to fill gaps in surfaces.
Apply mathematical models of financial or business conditions.
Apply mathematical principles or statistical approaches to solve problems in scientific or applied fields.
Apply mortar.
Apply multiple teaching methods.
Apply new technologies to improve work processes.
Apply paint to surfaces.
Apply parting agents or other solutions to molds.
Apply protective coverings to objects or surfaces near work areas.
Apply protective or decorative finishes to workpieces or products.
Apply sealants or other protective coatings.
Apply solutions to hair for therapeutic or cosmetic purposes.
Apply solutions to production equipment.

Apply water or solutions to fabrics or apparel.
Appraise environmental impact of regulations or policies.
Appraise property values.
Apprehend criminal suspects.
Approve expenditures.
Arbitrate disputes between parties to resolve legal conflicts.
Arrange artwork, products, or props.
Arrange childcare or educational settings to ensure physical safety of children.
Arrange collective bargaining agreements.
Arrange delivery of goods or services.
Arrange facility schedules.
Arrange food for serving.
Arrange insurance coverage.
Arrange items for use or display.
Arrange maintenance activities.
Arrange physical or mental health services for clients.
Arrange services or reservations for patrons.
Arrange tables or dining areas.
Assemble electrical components, subsystems, or systems.
Assemble electrical or electronic equipment.
Assemble electromechanical or hydraulic systems.
Assemble equipment or components.
Assemble garments or textile products.
Assemble machine tools, parts, or fixtures.
Assemble mechanical components or machine parts.
Assemble metal or plastic parts or products.
Assemble metal structures.
Assemble precision electronics or optical equipment.
Assemble products or production equipment.
Assemble structural components.
Assemble temporary equipment or structures.
Assemble tires.
Assemble wood products.
Assess characteristics of fires.
Assess compliance with environmental laws.
Assess database performance.
Assess educational needs of students.
Assess equipment functioning.
Assess financial status of clients.
Assess individual or community needs for educational or social services.
Assess locations for potential green technology installations.
Assess patient work, living, or social environments.
Assess physical conditions of patients to aid in diagnosis or treatment.
Assess product or process usefulness.
Assess risks to business operations.
Assess skin or hair conditions.
Assess the cost effectiveness of products, projects, or services.
Assign class work to students.
Assign duties or work schedules to employees.
Assign resources or facilities to patrons or employees.
Assist chefs or caterers with food or drink preparation.
Assist clients in handling details of daily life.
Assist customers to ensure comfort or safety.
Assist customers with seating arrangements.
Assist disabled or incapacitated individuals.
Assist engineers or scientists with research.
Assist healthcare practitioners during examinations or treatments.
Assist healthcare practitioners during surgery.
Assist individuals with paperwork.
Assist individuals with special needs.
Assist motorists or pedestrians.
Assist other educational professionals with projects or research.

Assist others during emergencies.
Assist passengers during vehicle boarding.
Assist patients with daily activities.
Assist patients with hygiene or daily living activities.
Assist patrons with entering or exiting vehicles or other forms of transportation.
Assist practitioners to perform medical procedures.
Assist skilled construction or extraction personnel.
Assist students with special educational needs.
Attach decorative or functional accessories to products.
Attach equipment extensions or accessories.
Attach identification information to products, items or containers.
Attach rigging to objects so they can be moved.
Attend conferences or workshops to maintain professional knowledge.
Attend educational events to update medical knowledge.
Attend events to develop professional knowledge.
Attend training sessions or professional meetings to develop or maintain professional knowledge.
Attend training to learn new skills or update knowledge.
Audition for roles.
Audition or interview potential performers or staff members.
Authorize construction activities.
Authorize financial actions.
Authorize payments to settle legal disputes.
Balance receipts.
Block physical access to restricted areas.
Bolt objects into place.
Braze metal parts or components.
Break up rock, asphalt, or concrete.
Build agricultural structures.
Build construction forms or molds.
Build models, patterns, or templates.
Build production molds.
Calculate costs of goods or services.
Calculate data to inform organizational operations.
Calculate dimensions of workpieces, products, or equipment.
Calculate financial data.
Calculate geographic positions from survey data.
Calculate numerical data for medical activities.
Calculate requirements for equipment installation or repair projects.
Calculate shipping costs.
Calculate specific material, equipment, or labor requirements for production.
Calculate tax information.
Calculate weights, volumes or other characteristics of materials.
Calibrate equipment to specifications.
Calibrate scientific or technical equipment.
Capture or kill animals.
Care for animals.
Care for patients with mental illnesses.
Care for plants or animals.
Care for women during pregnancy and childbirth.
Cast molds of patient anatomies to create medical or dental devices.
Check data for recording errors.
Check physical condition of people or animals.
Check quality of diagnostic images.
Check quality of foods or supplies.
Choose optimal transportation routes or speeds.
Choreograph dances.
Classify materials according to standard systems.
Classify organisms based on their characteristics or behavior.
Clean building walls or flooring.
Clean equipment or facilities.

Clean equipment or supplies.
Clean equipment, parts, or tools to repair or maintain them in good working order.
Clean fabrics or apparel.
Clean facilities or equipment.
Clean facilities or sites.
Clean facilities or work areas.
Clean food preparation areas, facilities, or equipment.
Clean food service areas.
Clean furniture or fixtures.
Clean machinery or equipment.
Clean materials to prepare them for production.
Clean medical equipment or facilities.
Clean medical equipment.
Clean objects.
Clean patient rooms or patient treatment rooms.
Clean production equipment.
Clean surfaces in preparation for work activities.
Clean tableware.
Clean tools or equipment.
Clean vehicles or vehicle components.
Clean vessels or marine equipment.
Clean work areas or facilities.
Clean work areas.
Clean work sites.
Clean workpieces or finished products.
Clear equipment jams.
Climb equipment or structures to access work areas.
Climb ladders or vehicles to perform duties.
Coach others.
Code data or other information.
Collaborate on research activities with scientists or technical specialists.
Collaborate with healthcare professionals to plan or provide treatment.
Collaborate with law enforcement or security agencies to respond to incidents.
Collaborate with law enforcement or security agencies to share information.
Collaborate with other agencies and institutions to coordinate educational matters.
Collaborate with other professionals to assess client needs or plan treatments.
Collaborate with other professionals to develop education or assistance programs.
Collaborate with other teaching professionals to develop educational programs.
Collaborate with others in marketing activities.
Collaborate with others to determine design specifications or details.
Collaborate with others to determine production details.
Collaborate with others to determine technical details of productions.
Collaborate with others to develop or implement marketing strategies.
Collaborate with others to develop or refine designs.
Collaborate with others to prepare or perform artistic productions.
Collaborate with others to resolve information technology issues.
Collaborate with outside groups to develop programs or projects.
Collaborate with technical specialists to resolve design or development problems.
Collect archival data.
Collect biological specimens from patients.
Collect biological specimens.
Collect data about customer needs.

Collect data about project sites.
Collect deposits, payments or fees.
Collect dirty dishes or other tableware.
Collect environmental data or samples.
Collect evidence for legal proceedings.
Collect fares or payment from customers.
Collect geographical or geological field data.
Collect geological samples.
Collect information about clients.
Collect information about community health needs.
Collect information from people through observation, interviews, or surveys.
Collect medical information from patients, family members, or other medical professionals.
Collect payments for good or services.
Collect payments for goods or services.
Collect samples for analysis or testing.
Collect samples of materials or products for testing.
Collect samples of raw materials or finished products.
Communicate detailed medical information to patients or family members.
Communicate dining or order details to kitchen personnel.
Communicate green energy production information.
Communicate health and wellness information to the public.
Communicate organizational information to customers or other stakeholders.
Communicate organizational policies and procedures.
Communicate patient status to other health practitioners.
Communicate project information to others.
Communicate results of environmental research.
Communicate situation details to appropriate personnel.
Communicate technical information to suppliers, contractors, or regulatory agencies.
Communicate test or assessment results to medical professionals.
Communicate with clients about products, procedures, and policies.
Communicate with coworkers to coordinate installations or repairs.
Communicate with customers to resolve complaints or ensure satisfaction.
Communicate with government agencies.
Communicate with management or other staff to resolve problems.
Communicate with other construction or extraction personnel to discuss project details.
Communicate with other workers to coordinate activities.
Communicate with others to coordinate material handling or movement.
Communicate with others to coordinate vehicle movement.
Communicate with the public on environmental issues.
Compact materials to create level bases.
Compare physical characteristics of materials or products to specifications or standards.
Compile data or documentation.
Compile environmental or climatological data.
Compile geographic or related data.
Compile operational data.
Compile specialized bibliographies or lists of materials.
Compile technical information or documentation.
Complete documentation required by programs or regulations.
Compute debt repayment schedules.
Compute gaming wins and losses.
Conduct amusement or gaming activities.
Conduct anthropological or archaeological research.
Conduct climatological research.
Conduct diagnostic tests to determine patient health.
Conduct eligibility or selection interviews.

Conduct employee training programs.
Conduct environmental audits.
Conduct financial or regulatory audits.
Conduct gaming transactions.
Conduct health or safety training programs.
Conduct hearings to investigate legal issues.
Conduct historical research.
Conduct market research.
Conduct opinion surveys or needs assessments.
Conduct quantitative failure analyses of operational data.
Conduct research of processes in natural or industrial ecosystems.
Conduct research on social issues.
Conduct research to gain information about products or processes.
Conduct research to increase knowledge about medical issues.
Conduct research to inform art, designs, or other work.
Conduct scientific research of organizational behavior or processes.
Conduct surveys in organizations.
Conduct test runs of production equipment.
Conduct validation tests of equipment or processes.
Confer with clients to determine needs.
Confer with clients to discuss treatment plans or progress.
Confer with clients to exchange information.
Confer with court staff to clarify information.
Confer with coworkers to coordinate maintenance or cleaning activities.
Confer with coworkers to coordinate work activities.
Confer with coworkers to resolve equipment problems.
Confer with customers or designers to determine order specifications.
Confer with customers or users to assess problems.
Confer with family members to discuss client treatment plans or progress.
Confer with managers to make operational decisions.
Confer with organizational members to accomplish work activities.
Confer with other personnel to resolve design or operational problems.
Confer with other professionals to plan patient care.
Confer with others about financial matters.
Confer with others to conduct or arrange operational activities.
Confer with others to resolve production problems or equipment malfunctions.
Confer with personnel to coordinate business operations.
Confer with technical personnel to prepare designs or operational plans.
Configure computer networks.
Confiscate prohibited or dangerous items.
Connect cables or electrical lines.
Connect electrical components or equipment.
Connect hoses to equipment or machinery.
Connect hoses to equipment or piping.
Connect supply lines to production equipment or tools.
Construct customized assistive medical or dental devices.
Construct distinctive physical objects for artistic, functional, or commercial purposes.
Construct exhibits or parts of exhibits.
Construct patterns, templates, or other work aids.
Consult with others regarding safe or healthy equipment or facilities.
Contact current or potential customers to promote products or services.
Contract real estate to clients.
Control equipment that regulates vehicle traffic.

Control power supply connections.
Control prescription refills or authorizations.
Control pumps or pumping equipment.
Convert data among multiple digital or analog formats.
Cook foods.
Coordinate activities of food service staff.
Coordinate activities of production personnel.
Coordinate activities with suppliers, contractors, clients, or other departments.
Coordinate artistic activities.
Coordinate athletic or sporting events or activities.
Coordinate construction or installation activities.
Coordinate construction project activities.
Coordinate cross-disciplinary research programs.
Coordinate design activities.
Coordinate enforcement of laws or regulations.
Coordinate flight control or management activities.
Coordinate forestry or agricultural activities.
Coordinate legal schedules or activities.
Coordinate logistics for productions or events.
Coordinate logistics or other business operations.
Coordinate musical rehearsals or performances.
Coordinate operational activities with external stakeholders.
Coordinate operational activities.
Coordinate personnel recruitment activities.
Coordinate project activities with other personnel or departments.
Coordinate regulatory documentation activities.
Coordinate reporting or editing activities.
Coordinate resource procurement activities.
Coordinate safety or regulatory compliance activities.
Coordinate sales campaigns.
Coordinate shipping activities with external parties.
Coordinate software or hardware installation.
Coordinate special events or programs.
Coordinate student extracurricular activities.
Coordinate timing of food production activities.
Coordinate training activities.
Coordinate with external parties to exchange information.
Correspond with customers to answer questions or resolve complaints.
Counsel clients on mental health or personal achievement.
Counsel clients or patients regarding personal issues.
Counsel clients or patients with substance abuse issues.
Counsel clients regarding educational or vocational issues.
Counsel clients regarding interpersonal issues.
Counsel family members of clients or patients.
Count finished products or workpieces.
Count prison inmates or personnel.
Create advanced digital images of patients using computer imaging systems.
Create computer-generated graphics or animation.
Create construction or installation diagrams.
Create databases to store electronic data.
Create diagrams or blueprints for workpieces or products.
Create electrical schematics.
Create electronic data backup to prevent loss of information.
Create graphical representations of civil structures.
Create graphical representations of energy production systems.
Create graphical representations of industrial production systems.
Create graphical representations of mechanical equipment.
Create graphical representations of structures or landscapes.
Create images of data, locations, or products.
Create images or other visual displays.
Create maps.
Create marketing materials.

Create models of engineering designs or methods.
Create musical compositions, arrangements or scores.
Create new recipes or food presentations.
Create physical models or prototypes.
Create schematic drawings for electronics.
Create technology-based learning materials.
Cultivate land.
Cultivate lawns, turf, or gardens.
Cultivate micro-organisms for study, testing, or medical preparations.
Customize energy products or services to meet customer needs.
Customize financial products or services to meet customer needs.
Cut carpet, vinyl or other flexible materials.
Cut cooked or raw foods.
Cut fabrics.
Cut glass.
Cut industrial materials in preparation for fabrication or processing.
Cut materials according to specifications or needs.
Cut meat products.
Cut metal components for installation.
Cut openings in existing structures.
Cut tile, stone, or other masonry materials.
Cut trees or logs.
Cut wood components for installation.
Decontaminate equipment or sites to remove hazardous or toxic substances.
Decorate indoor or outdoor spaces.
Deliver items.
Deliver promotional presentations to current or prospective customers.
Demonstrate activity techniques or equipment use.
Demonstrate products to consumers.
Design alternative energy systems.
Design civil structures or systems.
Design computer modeling or simulation programs.
Design control systems for mechanical or other equipment.
Design costumes or cosmetic effects for characters.
Design electrical equipment or systems.
Design electromechanical equipment or systems.
Design electronic or computer equipment or instrumentation.
Design energy production or management equipment or systems.
Design energy-efficient equipment or systems.
Design energy-efficient vehicles or vehicle components.
Design environmental control systems.
Design healthcare-related software applications.
Design industrial equipment.
Design industrial processing systems.
Design integrated computer systems.
Design jewelry or decorative objects.
Design layout of art or product exhibits, displays, or promotional materials.
Design layouts for print publications.
Design materials for industrial or commercial applications.
Design medical devices or appliances.
Design micro- or nano-scale materials, devices, or systems.
Design psychological or educational treatment procedures or programs.
Design public or employee health programs.
Design research studies to obtain scientific information.
Design software applications.
Design structures or facilities.
Design systems to reduce harmful emissions.
Design templates or patterns.

Design tools, fixtures, or other devices for production equipment.
Design video game features or details.
Design water conservation systems.
Design websites or web applications.
Detain suspects or witnesses.
Determine appropriate locations for operations or installations.
Determine appropriate methods for data analysis.
Determine causes of operational problems or failures.
Determine construction project layouts.
Determine design criteria or specifications.
Determine food production methods.
Determine forestry techniques or methods.
Determine geographic coordinates.
Determine metal or plastic production methods.
Determine methods to minimize environmental impact of activities.
Determine operational compliance with regulations or standards.
Determine operational criteria or specifications.
Determine operational methods.
Determine operational procedures.
Determine presentation subjects or content.
Determine prices for menu items.
Determine pricing or monetary policies.
Determine production equipment settings.
Determine protocols for medical procedures.
Determine resource needs.
Determine technical requirements of productions or projects.
Determine the value of goods or services.
Determine types of equipment, tools, or materials needed for jobs.
Develop agricultural methods.
Develop artistic or design concepts for decoration, exhibition, or commercial purposes.
Develop biological research methods.
Develop business or financial information systems.
Develop business or market strategies.
Develop business relationships.
Develop collaborative relationships between departments or with external organizations.
Develop computer or information security policies or procedures.
Develop computer or information systems.
Develop computer or online applications.
Develop content for sales presentations or other materials.
Develop contingency plans to deal with organizational emergencies.
Develop daily schedules for children or families.
Develop data analysis or data management procedures.
Develop database parameters or specifications.
Develop detailed project plans.
Develop diagrams or flow charts of system operation.
Develop educational goals, standards, policies, or procedures.
Develop educational or training programs.
Develop educational policies.
Develop educational programs.
Develop emergency procedures.
Develop emergency response plans or procedures.
Develop environmental remediation or protection plans.
Develop environmental research methods.
Develop environmental sustainability plans or projects.
Develop equipment or component configurations.
Develop exercise or conditioning programs.
Develop financial analysis methods.
Develop financial or business plans.
Develop financial plans for clients.

Develop fire safety or prevention programs or plans.
Develop guidelines for system implementation.
Develop health assessment methods or programs.
Develop healthcare quality and safety procedures.
Develop information communication procedures.
Develop instructional materials.
Develop instructional objectives.
Develop library or archival databases.
Develop marketing plans or strategies for environmental initiatives.
Develop marketing plans or strategies.
Develop mathematical models of environmental conditions.
Develop medical treatment plans.
Develop methods of social or economic research.
Develop models of information or communications systems.
Develop new or advanced products or production methods.
Develop operating strategies, plans, or procedures for green or sustainable operations.
Develop operating strategies, plans, or procedures.
Develop operational methods or processes that use green materials or emphasize sustainability.
Develop organizational goals or objectives.
Develop organizational methods or procedures.
Develop organizational policies or programs.
Develop patient therapy programs.
Develop performance metrics or standards related to information technology.
Develop plans for programs or services.
Develop plans to manage natural or renewable resources.
Develop policies or procedures for archives, museums or libraries.
Develop procedures for data entry or processing.
Develop procedures for data management.
Develop procedures to evaluate organizational activities.
Develop professional relationships or networks.
Develop program goals or plans.
Develop promotional materials.
Develop promotional strategies for religious organizations.
Develop promotional strategies or plans.
Develop proposals for current or prospective customers.
Develop safety standards, policies, or procedures.
Develop scientific or mathematical models.
Develop software or applications for scientific or technical use.
Develop software or computer applications.
Develop specifications for computer network operation.
Develop specifications for new products or processes.
Develop specifications or procedures for website development or maintenance.
Develop strategies or programs for students with special needs.
Develop sustainable business strategies or practices.
Develop sustainable industrial or development methods.
Develop sustainable organizational policies or practices.
Develop technical methods or processes.
Develop technical or scientific databases.
Develop technical processes to improve the efficiency of biofuel production.
Develop technical specifications for systems or equipment.
Develop testing routines or procedures.
Develop theories or models of physical phenomena.
Develop tools to diagnose or assess needs.
Develop training materials.
Develop treatment plans for patients or clients.
Develop treatment plans that use non-medical therapies.
Develop working relationships with others to facilitate program activities.
Devise research or testing protocols.

Diagnose dental conditions.
Diagnose equipment malfunctions.
Diagnose medical conditions.
Diagnose neural or psychological disorders.
Dig holes or trenches.
Direct activities of agricultural, forestry, or fishery employees.
Direct activities of subordinates.
Direct administrative or support services.
Direct construction activities.
Direct construction or extraction personnel.
Direct courtroom activities or procedures.
Direct criminal investigations.
Direct department activities.
Direct design or development activities.
Direct emergency management activities.
Direct employee training programs.
Direct energy production or management activities.
Direct environmental development activities.
Direct equipment maintenance or repair activities.
Direct facility maintenance or repair activities.
Direct financial operations.
Direct fire fighting or prevention activities.
Direct fundraising or financing activities.
Direct funeral or mortuary activities.
Direct green energy production operations.
Direct healthcare delivery programs.
Direct industrial production activities.
Direct installation activities.
Direct law enforcement activities.
Direct maintenance and repair activities in green energy production facilities.
Direct maintenance or repair activities.
Direct material handling or moving activities.
Direct medical science or healthcare programs.
Direct natural resources extraction projects.
Direct natural resources management or conservation programs.
Direct operational or production activities.
Direct operations of correctional facilities.
Direct organizational operations, projects, or services.
Direct passenger or freight transport activities.
Direct productions or performances.
Direct quality control activities.
Direct sales, marketing, or customer service activities.
Direct scientific activities.
Direct security operations.
Direct surveying activities.
Direct technical activities or operations.
Direct vehicle traffic.
Disassemble equipment for maintenance or repair.
Disassemble equipment to inspect for deficiencies.
Disburse funds from clients accounts to creditors.
Discuss account status or activity with customers or patrons.
Discuss business strategies, practices, or policies with managers.
Discuss child development and behavior with parents or guardians.
Discuss design or technical features of products or services with technical personnel.
Discuss designs or plans with clients.
Discuss goods or services information with customers or patrons.
Discuss performance, complaints, or violations with supervisors.
Discuss problems or issues with supervisors.
Discuss production content and progress with others.
Discuss service options or needs with clients.
Discuss student progress with parents or guardians.

Dismantle equipment or temporary structures.
Dismantle heavy equipment or machinery.
Display student work.
Dispose of biomedical waste in accordance with standards.
Dispose of hazardous materials.
Dispose of trash or waste materials.
Distribute incoming mail.
Distribute instructional or library materials.
Distribute materials to employees or customers.
Distribute promotional literature or samples to customers.
Distribute resources to patrons or employees.
Distribute supplies to workers.
Document client health or progress.
Document design or development procedures.
Document design or operational test results.
Document events or evidence, using photographic or audiovisual equipment.
Document information related to legal proceedings.
Document legal or regulatory information.
Document lesson plans.
Document network-related activities or tasks.
Document operational activities.
Document operational procedures.
Document organizational or operational procedures.
Document technical design details.
Document technical specifications or requirements.
Document test results.
Document work hours or activities.
Download data.
Draft legislation or regulations.
Draw detailed or technical illustrations.
Draw guide lines or markings on materials or workpieces using patterns or other references.
Drill holes in construction materials.
Drill holes in earth or rock.
Drill holes in parts, equipment, or materials.
Drive passenger vehicles.
Drive trucks or other vehicles to or at work sites.
Drive trucks or truck-mounted equipment.
Drive vehicles to transport individuals or equipment.
Drive vehicles to transport patrons.
Edit audio or video recordings.
Edit documents.
Edit written materials.
Educate clients on financial planning topics.
Educate the public about fire safety or prevention.
Embalm corpses.
Encourage patients during therapeutic activities.
Encourage patients or clients to develop life skills.
Encourage students.
Enforce rules or policies governing student behavior.
Enforce rules or regulations.
Engage patients in exercises or activities.
Engrave designs, text, or other markings onto materials, workpieces, or products.
Enter codes or other information into computers.
Enter commands, instructions, or specifications into equipment.
Enter information into databases or software programs.
Enter patient or treatment data into computers.
Entertain public with comedic or dramatic performances.
Escort prisoners to courtrooms, prisons, or other facilities.
Establish business management methods.
Establish interpersonal business relationships to facilitate work activities.
Establish nursing policies or standards.
Establish operational policies.
Establish organizational guidelines or policies.

Establish rules or policies governing student behavior.
Establish standards for medical care.
Establish standards for products, processes, or procedures.
Establish treatment goals.
Establish work standards.
Estimate construction project costs.
Estimate construction project labor requirements.
Estimate cost or material requirements.
Estimate costs for labor or materials.
Estimate costs for projects or productions.
Estimate costs of goods or services.
Estimate costs of products, services, or materials.
Estimate costs or terms of sales.
Estimate demand for products or services.
Estimate green project costs.
Estimate labor or resource requirements for forestry, fishing, or agricultural operations.
Estimate labor requirements.
Estimate maintenance service requirements or costs.
Estimate material requirements for production.
Estimate materials requirements for projects.
Estimate operational costs.
Estimate supplies, ingredients, or staff requirements for food preparation activities.
Estimate technical or resource requirements for development or production projects.
Estimate time or monetary resources needed to complete projects.
Estimate time requirements for development or production projects.
Evaluate applicable laws and regulations to determine impact on organizational activities.
Evaluate capabilities or training needs.
Evaluate characteristics of archival or historical objects.
Evaluate characteristics of equipment or systems.
Evaluate characteristics of individuals to determine needs or eligibility.
Evaluate civic projects or public policies.
Evaluate condition of properties.
Evaluate construction projects to determine compliance with external standards or regulations.
Evaluate current or prospective maintenance employees.
Evaluate data quality.
Evaluate designs or specifications to ensure quality.
Evaluate effectiveness of educational programs.
Evaluate effectiveness of personnel policies or practices.
Evaluate employee performance.
Evaluate energy production data.
Evaluate environmental impact of operational or development activities.
Evaluate environmental or sustainability projects.
Evaluate green operations or programs for compliance with standards or regulations.
Evaluate information related to legal matters in public or personal records.
Evaluate log quality.
Evaluate logistics methods to reduce environmental impact.
Evaluate new technologies or methods.
Evaluate patient functioning, capabilities, or health.
Evaluate patient outcomes to determine effectiveness of treatments.
Evaluate performance of applicants, trainees, or employees.
Evaluate performance of educational staff.
Evaluate personnel practices to ensure adherence to regulations.
Evaluate plans or specifications to determine technological or environmental implications.
Evaluate potential of products, technologies, or resources.

Evaluate potential problems in home or work environments of clients.
Evaluate program effectiveness.
Evaluate project designs to determine adequacy or feasibility.
Evaluate projects to determine compliance with technical specifications.
Evaluate quality of food ingredients or prepared foods.
Evaluate quality of materials or products.
Evaluate quality of plants or crops.
Evaluate reports or designs to determine work needs.
Evaluate scholarly materials.
Evaluate skills of athletes or performers.
Evaluate student work.
Evaluate technical data to determine effect on designs or plans.
Evaluate the characteristics of green technologies.
Evaluate the effectiveness of counseling or educational programs.
Evaluate training programs, instructors, or materials.
Evaluate treatment options to guide medical decisions.
Evaluate utility of software or hardware technologies.
Examine animals to detect illness, injury or other problems.
Examine characteristics or behavior of living organisms.
Examine condition of property or products.
Examine crime scenes to obtain evidence.
Examine debris to obtain information about causes of fires.
Examine documents to verify adherence to requirements.
Examine financial records or processes.
Examine financial records to ensure compliance with policies or regulations.
Examine financial records.
Examine marketing materials to ensure compliance with policies or regulations.
Examine medical instruments or equipment to ensure proper operation.
Examine mouth, teeth, gums, or related facial structures.
Examine patients to assess general physical condition.
Examine personal documentation to ensure that it is valid.
Examine physical characteristics of gemstones or precious metals.
Examine product information to ensure compliance with regulations.
Examine records or other types of data to investigate criminal activities.
Exchange information with colleagues.
Execute sales or other financial transactions.
Explain engineering drawings, specifications, or other technical information.
Explain financial information to customers.
Explain medical procedures or test results to patients or family members.
Explain project details to the general public.
Explain regulations, policies, or procedures.
Explain technical medical information to patients.
Explain technical product or service information to customers.
Explain use of products or services.
Fabricate devices or components.
Fabricate medical devices.
Fabricate parts or components.
Fabricate products or components using machine tools.
Feed materials or products into or through equipment.
Feed patients.
File documents or records.
Fill cracks, imperfections, or holes in products or workpieces.
Finish concrete surfaces.
Fit eyeglasses, contact lenses, or other vision aids.
Fit patients for assistive devices.
Follow protocols or regulations for healthcare activities.

Follow safety procedures for vehicle operation.
Forecast economic, political, or social trends.
Format digital documents, data, or images.
Gather customer or product information to determine customer needs.
Gather financial records.
Gather information about work conditions or locations.
Gather information for news stories.
Gather information in order to provide services to clients.
Gather medical information from patient histories.
Gather organizational performance information.
Gather physical survey data.
Give medications or immunizations.
Greet customers, patrons, or visitors.
Grind parts to required dimensions.
Groom wigs or hairpieces.
Guard facilities.
Guide class discussions.
Guide patrons on tours.
Handle caskets.
Handle luggage or other possessions for patrons.
Harvest agricultural products.
Heat material or workpieces to prepare for or complete production.
Help clients get needed services or resources.
Help patrons use library or archival resources.
Hire farming, fishing or forestry workers.
Hire personnel.
Hold patients to ensure proper positioning or safety.
Host events.
Identify actions needed to bring properties or facilities into compliance with regulations.
Identify environmental concerns.
Identify implications for cases from legal precedents or other legal information.
Identify information technology project resource requirements.
Identify investment opportunities or strategies.
Identify new applications for existing technologies.
Identify opportunities for green initiatives.
Identify opportunities to improve operational efficiency.
Identify potential customers.
Identify strategic business investment opportunities.
Identify sustainable business practices.
Ignite fuel to activate heating equipment.
Immerse objects or workpieces in cleaning or coating solutions.
Immunize patients.
Implement advanced life support techniques.
Implement advertising or marketing initiatives.
Implement design or process improvements.
Implement financial decisions.

Implement organizational process or policy changes.
Implement security measures for computer or information systems.
Implement therapeutic programs to improve patient functioning.
Implement transportation changes to reduce environmental impact.
Incorporate green features into the design of structures or facilities.
Inform individuals or organizations of status or findings.
Inform medical professionals regarding patient conditions and care.
Inform others about laws or regulations.
Inform the public about policies, services or procedures.
Inform viewers, listeners, or audiences.
Inspect aircraft or aircraft components.
Inspect areas for compliance with sanitation standards.
Inspect buildings or grounds to determine condition.
Inspect cargo areas for cleanliness or condition.
Inspect cargo to ensure it is properly loaded or secured.
Inspect cargo to identify potential hazards.
Inspect communications or broadcasting equipment.
Inspect completed work to ensure proper functioning.
Inspect completed work to ensure proper installation.
Inspect condition of natural environments.
Inspect condition or functioning of facilities or equipment.
Inspect electrical or electronic systems for defects.
Inspect equipment or facilities to determine condition or maintenance needs.
Inspect equipment or systems.
Inspect equipment or tools to be used in construction or excavation.
Inspect equipment to ensure proper functioning.
Inspect equipment to ensure safety or proper functioning.
Inspect equipment to locate or identify electrical problems.
Inspect facilities for cleanliness.
Inspect facilities or equipment to ensure specifications are met.
Inspect facilities or sites to determine if they meet specifications or standards.
Inspect facilities to ensure compliance with fire regulations.
Inspect facilities to ensure compliance with safety, quality, or service standards.
Inspect facilities to ensure compliance with security or safety regulations.
Inspect facilities, equipment or supplies to ensure conformance to standards.
Inspect facilities.
Inspect finished products to locate flaws.
Inspect finishes of workpieces or finished products.

Go back through all of these items, highlight or circle those Work Activities you are familiar with, would like to work with or want to know more about.

If you want to know more about an item, use the O*NET system and get a job profile or report for a job that uses it. Then consider doing an Informational Interview with someone who does it for a living. Can't find one? Use your network.

Problem Solving

In this section, we'll give you practice solving career and life problems. First, we'll present five Job and Career seeking problems for you to solve. We'll solve the first and leave the other two to you. It is easier to solve someone else's problems than your own because you are outside of the problem and can be objective. It still gives you good problem-solving practice.

After that, we'll move on to a series of "life's little" problems for you to think about. These are problems that happen to us all and when we're in the middle of it, it is hard to think of an answer or how to respond or handle it. If you think about it when there is no pressure on you at all, it gives you the chance to "see it coming" but deal with it

To assist you, we are putting the Problem Solving Model on a page of it's own at the end of this chapter. Use it now or anytime you are struggling with a problem.

Problem Solving Example 1:

The situation: A 35 year old person has been out of work for a long time. They are a high school graduate, married with children. Their spouse works but money is tight. Their job was in a factory assembly job. They have applied for several factory jobs but haven't been hired. No substance use or abuse issues. Not a veteran.

1) Identify the problem: We'll assume the want and need a job. Is this one problem? A group of problems? It's certainly important.

2) Resources: Do they have a current resume? Do they have difficulty with completing applications? Do they have a car? How far are they willing to travel? Have they visited MI Works? Do they use Pure Michigan Talent Connect? Have they identified their skills? Have they practiced interviewing with a Career Development Facilitator? Have they looked at Labor Market information to see what jobs pay in the range they would like to make or explored jobs that match their interests? Have they checked their references? Do they need training to find a job with better long term prospects?

3) Alternatives: Lots of alternatives. There is pressure to get started on a job, asap but getting a good one and keeping it might take longer. Might want to consider some options and looking at this as a three-parter:
   1) short term options (less than three months): Under short term options, spending time with MI Works staff to see what jobs they are already qualified for, and have interests that match. Review and sharpen resume, interviewing skills, application completing. Use resources to pursue job leads, within their geographical range. Consider taking "stop loss" job.
   2) medium term options (three months to a year): Accept "stop-loss" but plan to spend more time in career research to plan a better long term job with stability.
   3) long term options (over a year): Consider training/education to get job that offers long term stability and income that fits long term plans.

4) Pick an alternative: Since they need a job sooner rather than later, plan to spend 3-4 hours per day at SEMCA-MIWorks office. Apply for program services that enlist the assistance of

a Career Development Facilitator (CDF) and maintain close contact. Join Job Club. Use Pure Michigan Talent Connect and other online resources too.

5) Implement alternative: Immediately - register with SEMCA-MIWorks. Attend orientation session. Get familiar with all of the resources available there. Clear up job seeking barriers, re-start informed Job Hunt, including self-marketing in interviews.

6) Evaluate results: Got five interviews in first month, one offer for stop loss job. Followed up with all jobs, learned they had a problem with one reference, slightly "bad fit" for jobs applied for.

7) Not satisfied with results. Start problem solving sequence over again with new information. Found a new reference for their resume. Made adjustments to job targets.

You probably saw lots of options and other issues they have, right? That's okay, in fact it is better than okay, that's great!

Here's another one, this time, it's for you to work on and work out.

Problem Solving Example #2:

You are a "late-in-life", 50-something who has just lost a job you've had for the past 17 years. You worked for an auto supplier who outsourced your entire company to an offshore supplier. You live in a smaller town and now there are 300 of you all unemployed in one fell swoop. Your kids are grown but the last one is in college. Your spouse does have a part time job. You have a two-year degree in electronics which is how you eventually got your job at the supplier, where you worked as a repair technician. What should you do? Where do you start?

Identify the problem(s): _____

_____

_____

_____

_____

_____

Resources: _____

_____

_____

_____

_____

Alternatives: _____

_____

_____

_____

_____

_____

Pick an alternative (one or more): _____

_____
_____
_____
_____
_____

Implement alternative(s): _____
_____
_____
_____
_____
_____

Evaluate results: _____
_____
_____
_____
_____
_____

Satisfied?: _____
_____
_____
_____
_____
_____

Problem Solving Example #3:

You were a "stay at home, mom". You have two teenagers at home and your husband left you to live with his new "partner". You are a high school graduate but never had a job. You got married right out of high school. Your oldest is away at college, the youngest two are at home. Your husband has agreed to pay child support but you won't have enough to live on. What should you do? Where do you start?

Identify the problem(s): _____
_____
_____
_____
_____

Resources: _____
_____
_____
_____
_____
_____

Alternatives: _____

_____

_____

_____

_____

_____

Pick an alternative (one or more): _____

_____

_____

_____

_____

_____

Implement alternative(s): _____

_____

_____

_____

_____

_____

Evaluate results: _____

_____

_____

_____

_____

_____

Satisfied?: _____

_____

_____

_____

_____

_____

Problem Solving Example #4:

You are a "kid" just out of high school. You got along well but didn't really light up with any of the things the other kids were talking about doing after they graduated. You didn't feel like college was for you. You didn't want to join the military. You don't have a job. You live at home but your parents are on your back to "do something besides play video games and be on your computer all day and all night". What should you do? Where do you start?

Identify the problem(s): _____

_____

_____

_____

_____

Resources: _____

_____
_____
_____
_____
_____

Alternatives: _____

_____
_____
_____
_____
_____

Pick an alternative (one or more): _____

_____
_____
_____
_____
_____

Implement alternative(s): _____

_____
_____
_____
_____
_____

Evaluate results: _____

_____
_____
_____
_____
_____

Satisfied: _____

_____
_____
_____
_____
_____

Problem Solving Example #5 (three options to pick from):

You are an ex-offender (in other words, you committed and were convicted of a felony.). Or, you are an alcoholic or substance abuser who has just completed treatment. Or, you are an alcoholic or substance user/abuser and haven't gone into treatment.

What should you do? Where do you start?

Identify the problem(s): _____

_____

_____

_____

_____

_____

Resources: _____

_____

_____

_____

_____

_____

Alternatives: _____

_____

_____

_____

_____

_____

Pick an alternative (one or more): _____

_____

_____

_____

_____

_____

Implement alternative(s): _____

_____

_____

_____

_____

_____

Evaluate results: _____

_____

_____

_____

_____

_____

Satisfied?: _____

_____

_____

_____

_____

What will you do, if it happens to you?

- A close relative has been rushed to the hospital, what do you do?
- A close relative is going to be in the hospital a few days and will need your support at home for a few weeks, what do you do?
- A close relative will need you to take them for medical treatment, 2 x a week for an unknown length of time, what do you do?
- A co-worker is taunting you, what do you do?
- You are just told you have to work a holiday and you had plans, what do you do?
- You are feeling sick, what do you do?
- Your boss or someone else gives you really bad news, enough to make you very angry, very very angry. Should you:
  - Tell'em off, grab your stuff and go?
  - File a grievance with HR?
  - Call the government because your rights were violated?
  - Suck it up?

Some workplace problems, events and actions that you might encounter:
  - Your boss will yell at you
  - Your lunch will be stolen
  - A co-worker may make fun of you
  - You may be falsely accused of something
  - You have an emergency and need to leave.
  - You get sick
  - A co-worker doesn't come in and you have to do extra, maybe a lot of extra work
  - You screw up
  - You're going to be late.

Off the job, Job Support Problems:
- transportation
- child care.

What other problems have you run into on the job?
- Did you see better solutions then the one you used?
- Did you learn from your mistakes?
- Can you learn from your mistakes?

More problems:
- You want to work, to get a job. Where do you start?
- You need help identifying interests that tie into jobs.
- You need help identifying how skills, abilities, education and what they jobs match to.
- You need help with knowledge of opportunities.
- You need help with resume or interview skills.
- You need help with job leads.

What should you do if those things happen to you?

Problem Solving Model

1. Identify the Problem
    1. Is it really just one big problem? If so, what is it?
    2. If it is a multi-part problem, what are they?
    3. If is a bunch of problems, what are they?
    4. How big a problem is it? Is it important to solve it right away or can it wait?

2. Review Resources
    1. Have you seen this problem before? How did you solve it then? Can you use the same solution?
    2. If it is a new problem, is it like any problem you've seen before? Would a similar solution work now?
    3. What might it take to solve this problem? Time, money, outside assistance?

3. Generate Alternatives
    1. What options do you have?

4. Select Alternative
    1. Pick one of the options, (usually the most efficient, economical, available, and likely to succeed, is a good starting point).

5. Implement Alternative
    1. Give it a try.

6. Evaluate Results
    1. See what happens.
    2. How did it work out for you?
    3. Was the outcome satisfactory or could it have gone better? Was it good enough? Was it much better than you thought?

7. Did the Solution Work?
    1. Yes - you are done. Yay!
    2. No - start over again, this time with new information, new insights.

Identify the problem(s): _____

_____

_____

_____

_____

_____

Resources: _____

_____

_____

_____

_____

_____

Alternatives: _____

_____

_____

_____

_____

_____

Pick an alternative (one or more): _____

_____

_____

_____

_____

_____

Implement alternative(s): _____

_____

_____

_____

_____

Evaluate results: _____

_____

_____

_____

_____

Satisfied?: _____

_____

_____

_____

_____

Goals

Date: _____

On this page write down your answers to the following statements. There are no right or wrong answers. As long as you know what you mean, write it down. You don't have to come up with ten items for each one, but why not? You can come back and add more later.

Do try to be specific. For example, if you want a new car, what kind of car, what year, model, color? Make these goals as clear as possible. Once you have written them down, look at them everyday for two weeks. Then put them away and let the power of your subconscious help you obtain them. Save them and look at them in one year, five years, ten. See how many you attain. Our subconscious is a powerful tool in helping us get what we want.

10 Things I Want: _____
_____
_____
_____
_____
_____
_____
_____
_____
_____

10 Things I'd like to Do: _____
_____
_____
_____
_____
_____
_____
_____
_____
_____

10 Things I'd like to Change: _____
_____
_____
_____
_____
_____
_____
_____
_____
_____

10 Places I'd like to Go: _____

_____
_____
_____
_____
_____
_____
_____
_____
_____

10 Things I'd like to Be: _____

_____
_____
_____
_____
_____
_____
_____
_____
_____

Job and Career Goal Attainment

Recall goal attainment is a type of problem solving and that the first step of problem solving is to define the problem. What is your goal? What is your most rewarding job or career goal?

Here are some examples:
1) I want to be in the skilled trades as an electrician because I like making things work and to light up networks.
2) I want to be a veterinarian because I love animals.
3) I want to sell medical equipment to hospitals because I want to help people.
4) I want to be a realtor because I want to help people find the right home.
5) I want to be a clerk in a government office because I am good a record keeping.

Here is an example of "not a job goal", "I just want a job." That is far too vague. If you do not have a clear job or career goal, that is your starting point. That is the first goal to attain, "get a job goal" Solve that one first.

In the book, "It's Your future" and in this workbook, we performed exercises that should help you state your goal in a few words or sentences. Look at the work you did with O*NET and My Next Move as sources of job and career specific information. Look at and incorporate the work you did in the "Why People Work" and "Why People Volunteer" exercises. All of that material can contribute to help clarify for you your most rewarding job and career goals.

If you did select one or more potential job or career targets based on your research using O*NET, did you check to see if the values O*NET indicated were similar to those you selected in the "Why People Work" and "Why People Volunteer" exercises? Those elements should be present in any rewarding job goal you have. Those are things you should look for in the work place. For example, if you selected "helping people" as important to you in those two exercises, does your job target or career target include that aspect?

Once you know what you want, what goal you want to obtain, you then work on getting from where you are to your goal. Your starting point is where you are now and your endpoint is where you are going. What steps do you need to take to get there?

What alternatives do you have available to you in order to reach your goal? What steps will you need to take? What obstacles will you have to overcome? What barriers will you have to break though? Often, we do not and cannot anticipate these obstacles and barriers, that is not a problem. The bigger issue is bringing enough motivation and perseverance to the goal attainment to overcome them.

If you have a starting point and and endpoint, you can determine the steps you will need to take and put them in the correct order to get to your goal. All that is left is for you to take action.
Once you've started on the goal attainment path, you may have to make adjustments but that is typical.

If you have identified steps to take on you goal attainment path, practice the "Do List Habit".

The Do List Habit:

Today:
Write down things you want to do or that need to get done tomorrow.

Tomorrow:
Do as many of those things that you can (Try to do the most important things first.)
Cross of those you did do.
Put the date on the list and put it away (Documentation. Remember?)
Make a new list before the day ends.

Once a week or once a month, look at the the things you accomplished.

When should you alter your course or change your plan? When it is clearly not working.

Remember these things:
• Captains Chart Course and follow it, to get from where they are to where they want to be.
  You are the Captain of your life.
• Fishermen Fish
• Hunters Hunt
• Farmers Farm
• Workers Work
• What goals does your behavior reveal?

Organized Plan

Now that we've spent time on where you are and on your goals, let's talk about a "plan".

Webster defines it as a "set of actions that have been thought of as a way to do or achieve something" and as "something that a person intends to do".

A plan, formal or informal, is an idea before it is anything else. An idea of how you want things to turn out, what you want to accomplish, where you want to go, what you want to have.

Plans start with an outcome, where you would like to finish, a description in some form of one or more goals.

Some examples of outcomes are: teach English in a high school, build a new house, drive to Mt. Rushmore, bake a cake.

A plan will usually include a description of what it will take to obtain that outcome. Sometimes you will even need more than one set of plans to obtain an outcome. For example to build a new house requires "plans" for the actual construction as well as "plans" to finance the construction.

Plans sometimes include the starting point, as in locating where you are on a map in order to work out a plan to arrive at Mt Rushmore.

An organized plan will identify where you are, where you want to be (goal) and what it will take to get there and the order you need to do things in. It will identify the gaps between where you are and identify ways to bridge the gaps.

Example 1:

Long Range Goal: Teach English in a high school.
Starting point: no college education but high school graduate.
Gap: College education
Gap: Finances for college education.
Short term goals:
Analyze college opportunities (which colleges at what cost and probability of attaining Long Range Job Goal)
Identify sources of finance for education
Apply to college(s)
Get accepted and work your butt off to complete college and get job.

Plans do not have to be highly formalized and highly detailed to work out. They do need to be clear enough to guide your actions and activities to move from your starting point through to your goal.

Sometimes they are very simple. Baking a cake requires following a set of steps on the back of a cake mix box, or in a recipe book, in the proper order with the proper ingredients.

Sometimes they can be quite complex, as the plans for building a modern jet airplane or aircraft carrier would be.

Since the focus of this Workbook, and the book it accompanies ("It's Your Future"), are about your Most Rewarding Job and Career, you will find that same range for plans, from simple and informal to complex and formal, applies to your planning.

The key elements of your Job and Career plans will be: 1) to understand yourself in a work context, 2) to be knowledgeable about your real work opportunities, 3) to understand the overlap and intersection of job hunting with job openings.

Businesses and employers need employees, that's a given. Your plan needs to identify those businesses and employers who need you and to help them hire you.

If you do not know how to help them hire you, turn to the Marketing Planning sections of the book and the workbook. Review the material on Interviewing too.

If you do not know how to get them to interview you, turn to the sections on Resumes, Applications, Informational Interviewing, and Marketing.

If you don't know who would hire you and what your real work opportunities are, turn to the sections on O*NET, and My Next Move in the book and Marketing.

If you don't know who you are in the job and work context, turn to the O*NET sections and learn about yourself.

Know who you are.

Know you're potential.

Know what work you can do now, with who you are today, and what work you can do, who you can be with more experience, education, skill, and training.

Know what the basics are in any job search and how to do them well.

Take action and take charge.

Informational Interviewing:

There are three phases to Informational Interviewing: 1) Making contact, 2) The Interview, and 3) Follow-up.

Before you conduct an informational interview, you should have a purpose for doing it. Ask yourself, why do I want to do this interview? Obviously, you want information. It should be information that you cannot obtain through outside resources. You need "inside" information. You want information that only someone who is doing the job can provide, their point of view, their insight, their knowledge. You may turn this interviewee into a contact for you to use in the future, as a resource.

Before you make that first contact, think about what you want to learn. That will not only form the basis for the interview but also for your initial contact with the interviewee.

Suppose you think you could be a Water Quality Inspector. You've done some research and think you have the qualifications for an entry level job. Wouldn't it be helpful in your career planning to actually speak to one, especially where they work? You'd have a chance to see what the environment was like plus have the opportunity to ask questions of importance to you.

There are three forms of initial contact you can make with a potential interviewee; 1) by email, 2) by letter, 3) by phone. It is most difficult to get an appointment to conduct an informational interview by phone without first sending either an email or a letter. If you send one of those the potential interviewee will understand why you are calling.

Assuming you have done enough research to have identified a specific person to contact, here are some aids for you to use to successfully make contact, interview and follow-up.

Structure for an email:

To: _____ (<=== the person you want to interview.)
Subject: _____ (<=== "topic) OR subject may be
Subject: Referred to you by _____ (the name of a person who has referred you).

The topic in the "subject line" could be their job, job title, their company or employer, an article they wrote or any other thing that gives them a point of reference as to your subject and does not make them think "spam" or "job hunter".

Email Body (content)

Here you want to state what your purpose in contacting them is. Don't start with "I want to meet with you and interview you." Your purpose is to learn something from them, as we said a few paragraphs back. What is it about the person, what they've done or are doing that makes them someone you want to speak with? Set the stage then ask for a brief meeting at a time convenient for them, and a phone number to call them at.

Close with your name and number.

Example:

I am writing to you because I read about your works on Robotics in an article in last months Robotics Monthly. I am a beginning robotics engineer and share your interest. Would you be willing to talk to me about your article and your work? May I have a phone number I can reach you at to speak with you?

My name is Joe E. Jones and I can be reached at 555.678.4321

Thank you.

Try filling in this "Email":

To: _____

Subject: _____

Text:_____

_____

_____

_____

_____

_____

_____

_____

_____

_____

_____

_____

A letter is structured a little differently but will conform to an email in that it will state why you are contacting them specifically, and then a request to meet with them.

Example:

Sandra Smith, Director
Research & Development Laboratories
MedRed Inc
1234 Fifth Street
Fiction City, MI 48999

Dear Ms. Smith;

I am writing to you because of my interest in the development of new medical devices. My research revealed that MedRed is an international leader in Research & Development of medical devices and that you are a key individual in their success.

I am sure you have a very busy schedule but I would like to arrange a brief meeting with you to discuss your own growth and development to become the leader you are. We could even meet during a lunch period if that would be convenient for you.

I plan to call you on Monday, between 3:00 pm and 4:00 pm to make arrangements with you or you may feel free to call me at 555-333-2424 anytime.

Thank you so very much and I look forward to meeting you.

Sincerely

Melanie T Johnson

You may not succeed in making arrangements for an informational interview on your first try, or second or even third but do not despair. You will find that many people are open to meeting with you and discussing themselves. It may take a little practice on your part, just don't give up. They have something you want, inside information.

Once you have an Informational Interview set-up, what are you going to ask and what else should you consider. We'll start with other considerations first.

Make sure you know the location of where you will meet with this person. Plan on dressing up, looking as though the first impression you're going to make could land you a great job. It happens. Bring a resume, just in case. Do not treat the interview lightly. This person is being kind enough to give you their most precious assets, their time and their knowledge. Depending on who they are, they have worked hard to get where they are, made their share of sacrifices and their time is in demand. Treat them with respect.

What are you going to ask? Here's a list of starter questions than you can use. Take a notebook of some form with the questions you want to ask written down and room to write down their answers and to take notes not only on what they say but also about the environment if you want to learn about "where they work".

Interview Starter Questions:
- How did you get started (in robotics, or making documentaries or doing research and development)?
- When did you first get interested in ...?
- How long have you been doing this ...?
- What do you like most about your work?
- What do you like least about your work?
- What advice would you give someone who is interested in ...?
- What is the work like?
- Is there a typical day and what is it like?
- What are the prospects for someone entering the field today?
- What kind of training was required?
- What do employers look for in someone in this field?
- How much freedom do employees have to set their own work schedule?
- Does this company support further education and training opportunities?
- What are the companies core values?
- What determines success in this company?
- What determines success in this field?
- Do you work alone much of the time?
- Do you work with others much of the time?

- Are you part of a team?
- What's your role on the team?

If you asked the interviewee for a half-hour (or an hour) be sure to let them know that you are aware of having reached that point in time and offering to end the interview then. Many times the interviewee will have time to continue talking with you as long as they feel like it is being productive for you. Some people love talking about their jobs and will go and on. As long as you're getting your information, let them talk.

With practice you will become a skillful interviewer. The only way to get the practice is by doing it. Keep in mind that there are several useful benefits to doing so. One benefit is that you will become more relaxed in interviews and find that job interviews are less threatening. That will give you an advantage over other job candidates. A second benefit is that the person you interview may be in a position to recommend you for a job within their company or point you toward a job in their industry, or may identify resources you didn't know existed. That's why you interviewed them, isn't it, to learn what they know?

Okay, so you did it. You did your first Informational Interview. You learned a lot, and now you're back at home. What should you do with that new-found knowledge? Nothing, first you should write them a thank you letter, show a little gratitude to someone kind enough to give your their time and hard earned knowledge.

Sample letter:

Dear M_ _____;

I want to thank you for taking the time to meet with me on (<u>whatever day it was</u>). Your insights and information gave me a new appreciation and perspective on (their work, the company, etc).

I know how valuable your time is and appreciate the time (or state the hours) you spent with me.

If I can ever be of assistance or return the favor, do not hesitate to call on me. Again, thank you very much.

Sincerely

(Your name)
(Phone number)

When you type up this letter, include your address. If you did not leave a resume with them but think it is a good idea they have one, indicate that you've included it. If you can pinpoint one or two ideas they gave you that are of particular value, say it. We all like to hear that we've said something of value to another but so rarely hear it.

Interview Starter Questions:

How did you get started (in robotics, or making documentaries or doing research and development)? _____
_____
_____

When did you first get interested in ...? _____
_____
_____

How long have you been doing this ...? _____
_____
_____

What do you like most about your work? _____
_____
_____

What do you like least about your work? _____
_____
_____

What advice would you give someone who is interested in ...? _____
_____
_____

What is the work like? _____
_____
_____

Is there a typical day and what is it like? _____
_____
_____

What are the prospects for someone entering the field today? _____
_____
_____

What kind of training was required? _____
_____
_____

What do employers look for in someone in this field? _____
_____

How much freedom do employees have to set their own work schedule? _____

_____

_____

Does this company support further education and training opportunities? _____

_____

_____

What are the companies core values? _____

_____

_____

What determines success in this company? _____

_____

_____

What determines success in this field? _____

_____

_____

Do you work alone much of the time? _____

_____

_____

Do you work with others much of the time? _____

_____

_____

Are you part of a team? _____

_____

_____

What's your role on the team? _____

_____

_____

Add your own questions here:

_____

_____

Job Target Worksheet:

On the following pages are Job Target Worksheets.

Start by listing a job target and then list what critical elements, Tasks, Knowledge, etc, are most important on this job. You should be able to get a fairly clear picture by looking at the Department of Labor's O*NET occupational information (You could also simply print out the O*NET Summary Report).

You do not need to list all of the items within each element, simply those that are most important, especially as they relate to you. In other words, if the key task was: "Obtain information needed to complete legal documents, such as death certificates or burial permits" and you have experience that includes obtaining information needed to complete legal documents, especially for other people, be sure to list that item. If there are ten tasks listed for the job, you can list all ten.

The purpose of this form is to give you a comprehensive review of the job you are seeking, while at the same time surfacing information about you that relates to the job. Doing this gives you a clear picture of your strengths, and weaknesses, as they relate to this particular job.

Complete one of these for each of your Job Targets.

Job Target Worksheet

Job Target:_____

Tasks: _____
_____
_____
_____
_____
_____

Knowledge: _____
_____
_____
_____
_____
_____

Skills: _____
_____
_____
_____
_____
_____

Abilities: _____
_____
_____
_____
_____
_____

Work Activities: _____
_____
_____
_____
_____

Work Context: _____
_____
_____
_____
_____
_____

Job Zone: _____
_____

_____
_____
_____
_____

Education: _____
_____
_____
_____
_____
_____

Training: _____
_____
_____
_____
_____

Interests: _____
_____
_____
_____
_____

Work Styles: _____
_____
_____
_____
_____

Work Values: _____
_____
_____
_____
_____

Job History Worksheet

In this section you can create a Job History Worksheet, one for each job you've held. List the Employer, Job Title, Dates, and your Job Duties. Take a few minutes and add what you liked or disliked about that job and what was rewarding about it. Did you learn new skills or use new tools or technology?

You should already be thinking about what things you did on that job and for that employer, in light of the job you want and from a potential employers perspective.

List everything you can remember you did. Print that trial worksheet out (one per job target) and circle the items that are found in your top Job Target job descriptions you listed in the previous exercise.

You should plan on having one or more pages per job you've had.

At the top of each page, start by writing down the date range you worked at employer. It is best if you have the day, month and year you began and left each employer.

Note here that you don't have to follow this too rigorously, it is just a suggestion to help guide you. If you are more comfortable with a different arrangement of the information by all means tailor it to you.

Job History Worksheet

Employer: _____

Employer Address: _____
_____

Supervisor (include title and phone number): _____
_____

Date Started : _____ Date Ended: _____

Job Titles (starting, and each promotion, or transfer): _____
_____
_____

Job Duties (Tasks): _____
_____
_____
_____
_____

Tools & Technology: _____
_____
_____
_____
_____
_____

Knowledge, skills and abilities acquired and/or used: _____
_____
_____
_____
_____
_____

Likes, Dislikes, and what was rewarding? _____
_____
_____
_____
_____
_____
_____

Resumes:

Things in common with functional and chronological types of resume are the presentation of headings and your name. Your name should be in **bold** letters. Headings like **Work History**, too. Do not create a heading for "address" or "telephone number" or email addresses, simply put them below your name. It is neither especially correct nor incorrect to use a type-size larger for your name than everything else, like this **Johnson Q. Public** instead of this **Johnson Q. Public**.

You will typically see your address, telephone number and email address below your name. If your name is centered on the page, so are they, the key is to make that section appear harmonious, like this:

Johnson Q. Public
1745 North Territorial Road, Sometown, State 99999
Ph: 555.999.4673, Email: jqp@myhost.net

or like this if you are left-aligning:

Johnson Q. Public
1745 North Territorial Road, Sometown, State 99999
Ph: 555.999.4673, Email: jqp@myhost.net.

Is one method superior to another? Not really, do a little research and you'll find examples written both ways. What is more important, is the "look". One thing, if you center your name section, then center the headings, if you left align you name section, then left align the other sections. You want your resume to look harmonious.

Be sure to use a standard 1" margin, top, bottom, right and left. Don't squeeze the information to fit onto one page by cutting the margins down, it looks cheap and cheesy. It is better to use two pages than to squeeze things into one. If you use two pages, try to comfortably fill both. If you have enough information about you, especially as is related to the job, to require you to start a second page, then uncover and surface enough information to fill both pages without over-crowding. References can be as simple as: "Supplied upon request", or spelled out, which can use three to six lines for three references, four to eight if you provide four.

If you completed many of the exercises in the book and the workbook, you have lots of information about you that you can supply. Try to focus it as it will relate to your job objective but don't be above putting something in that also makes you a better candidate than the next person. It could be something that makes you a viable candidate not only for the job you apply for but to be promoted. Remember your resume is your "print" statement, your advertisement about you and how well you fit that job and that employer. Make it shine!

Now for the components of the two most common kinds of paper, "hard copy" resumes.

Components of a Chronological Resume:

1. Name

2. Address, Telephone Number and Email Address
3. Job Objective - Position Desired
4. Work Experience or Work History
5. Education and Training
6. Special Items;
    a. Skills
    b. Abilities
    c. Awards or Certifications
7. References

Components of a Functional Resume:

1. Name
2. Address, Telephone Number and Email Address
3. Job Objective - Position Desired
4. Highlighted Information
    a. Qualifications
    b. Professional Skills
5. Work History
6. Education and Training
7. Special Items:
    a. Professional Organizational Memberships
    b. Awards or Certifications
    c. Skills and Abilities
8. References.

When you encounter electronic resumes, as many government websites are using for job applications, you will provide the same information in whatever format they set up for you. Be prepared to fill-in their on-line form and to be asked many more questions than a resume would contain. Most permit you to work in sessions or small batches, so you won't have to complete them all at once.

It is now common for employers to have "uploading" mechanisms for you to submit an electronic resume. Your best bet is to have a functional type of resume in both Microsoft Word format and as a portable document file, or "pdf". Some employer systems can handle .txt or minimally formatted text files, fewer can handle an Apple Pages document. The standards for uploading are still changing and shifting but their goals are the same, get your resume into their system instead of on paper.

Some of these employers use "strippers" or "skimmers" to get at information quickly using computers to sort out viable from non-viable applicants. Which means some jobs you would be the best candidate for will not be offered because a computer didn't make the right choice. Life in the 21st century and why we think "in person" is best.

Sample Job Application Form

Position Applied for: _____ Date: _____

Personal Information

Last	First	MI	SSN:	DoB

Street Address		City	State	Zip

Home Phone	Cell phone	Email address

Are you entitled to work in the United States? Yes No

Have you been convicted of a felony or been incarcerated in connection with a felony in the past seven years? If yes, please explain>	Explanation

Are you a veteran? Yes No	Military Branch:	From	To
Discharge Type:	Discharge Rank:		

Expected Starting Wage:	When can you start?

Education

	Name - Location	Years Attended	Graduate?	Degree
High School				
College				
College				
Trade School				
Other				

List any applicable special skills, training or proficiencies:

Work History

Name:		Phone:	
Address			
Job Title		Supervisor	
Start Date:	End Date:	Dept	
Start Pay	End Pay	May we contact?	

Work History

Job Duties:

Promotions, awards, certification, additional training?

Work History

Name:		Phone:	
Address			
Job Title		Supervisor	
Start Date:	End Date:	Dept	
Start Pay	End Pay	May we contact?	

Job Duties:

Promotions, awards, certification, additional training?

Disclaimer - By signing, I hereby certify that the above information, to the best of my knowledge, is correct. I understand that falsification of this information may prevent me from being hired or lead to my dismissal if hired. I also provide consent for former employers to be contacted regarding work records.

Signature:	Date:

Telephone Contact Summary

For calls from employers

Now that your resume is in the hands of someone who can do something about it, and you've completed an application (possibly the day of the interview) it is time for more preparation. Keep this telephone contact summary by your phone or with you so that you are prepared for their call. You may get the information in any order, so be prepared!

Date: _____   Time: _____

Name of Person calling: _____

Phone Number: _____

Company: _____

Job Applied for: _____

Appointment Date and Time: _____

Interview location: _____

Interviewers Name: _____

Phone Number: _____

Special Directions (to the location, who to contact upon building entry):
_____
_____
_____

Where should I park?: _____
_____
_____

Anything else?: _____
_____
_____

Special Instructions (anything I need to bring with me?): _____
_____
_____
_____

Telephone Call Log

For Calls to Employers

Date: _____   Time: _____

Company: _____

Name of Person Called: _____

Phone Number: _____

Reason for Calling (Spell it out before you call. Were you calling to set up an Informational Interview, following up on a job application, heard about an opening, referred by someone, other?): _____
_____
_____
_____

Any key points you'd like to make to support your purpose, your reason for calling:
_____
_____

If the person you are trying to reach wasn't available, to whom did you speak?

Name: _____
Title: _____

Outcome: _____
_____
_____

Appointment Date and Time: _____

Interview location: _____

Special Directions (to the location, who to contact upon building entry and where to park):
_____
_____
_____

Special Instructions (anything I need to bring with me?): _____
_____

Interview Checklist

Double-check the following:

- Resume - extra copy to take with, reviewed to be ready to answer questions
- Appearance
    - Hair clean and in place.
        - Men facial hair trimmed or shaven?
    - Clothes clean, pressed, and job appropriate
        - Women avoid: too much cleavage, skirt too short, too much make-up?
    - Perfume or aftershave - none
    - Piercings removed, tattoo's covered?
    - Teeth, brushed, mouth rinsed
    - Smoke (cigar, cigarette, pipe, other) - don't, do not smell of smoke, period.
    - Gum chewing - don't.
    - Fidgety
    - Shoes shined.
- Travel (plan to be a wee bit early, about 15 minutes)
- Name of interviewer
- Job title and duties reviewed.
- Expect to sell to get the job (USP, STAR).

Remember employers are looking for people who:
• want to do the job
• can do the job
• are willing to do the job
• will be on time, reliably and dependably.
• will show up ready to work
• get along with others
• are trustworthy
• are affordable
• are worth investing in
• will stay.

• On the way in
    • Be On Time (15 minutes early)
    • Smile
    • Mind your manners
        • Don't sit until invited to
        • Don't remain seated when an interviewer enters the room if they weren't there when you were brought in
        • Greet everyone with a pleasant greeting
        • Say please and thank you
    • Turn off your cell phone before you enter the building (or at least silence it)
    • Calm yourself,
    • Remind yourself to listen and answer the question asked, and slow down.

Job Questions You Should Ask

Here are a number of questions that you might ask in an interview. They do not all fit or apply to every job. Highlight the ones that seem most appropriate to you and the job(s) you are seeking. Make a list of the top 10 questions in order of importance to you, and bring them to the job interview. It's okay to be prepared!

The Job - try to get as clear a picture as you can about the day-to-day duties of the job, the work you will be doing.

- What does a typical day look like?
- What are the most immediate projects that need to be addressed?
- Can you show me examples of projects I'd be working on?
- What are the skills and experiences you're looking for in an ideal candidate?
- What attributes does someone need to have in order to be really successful in this position?
- What types of skills is the team missing that you're looking to fill with a new hire?
- What are the biggest challenges that someone in this position would face?
- What sort of budget would I be working with?
- Is this a new role that has been created?
- Do you expect the main responsibilities for this position to change in the next six months to a year?
- Are you most interested in a candidate who works independently, on a team, cross-functionally, or through a combination of them all? Can you give me an example?
- How much travel is expected?
- How has this position evolved since it was created?
- How do you see this position contributing to the success of the organization?
- Is this a new position, or did someone leave? If someone left, why did they leave or what did they go on to do?
- What would you say are the three most important skills needed to excel in this position?
- What specific qualities and skills are you looking for in the job candidate?
- What are the duties and responsibilities of the position?
- What are some challenges that will face the person filling this position?
- What is the single largest problem facing your staff, and would I be in a position to help you solve this problem?

Training and Professional Development - You are on a path to obtain your next Most Rewarding Job and Career. Will this job help you get there?

- How will I be trained?
- What training programs are available to your employees?
- Are there opportunities for advancement or professional development?
- Would I be able to represent the company at industry conferences?
- Where have successful employees in this position progressed to?
- Does the company offer continued education and professional training?
- What is the typical career trajectory for a person in this position?
- What are the prospects for growth and advancement?

- Am I going to be a mentor or will I be mentored?

Your Performance - How will they measure your performance on the job? What goals are in place that you will be measured against and your performance evaluated?

- What are the most important things you'd like to see someone accomplish in the first 30, 60, and 90 days on the job?
- What are the performance expectations of this position over the first 12 months?
- What is the performance review process here? How often will I be formally reviewed?
- What metrics or goals will my performance be evaluated against?
- How will you judge my success?
- What will have happened six months from now that will demonstrate that I have met your expectations?
- What would success look like?
- What have past employees done to succeed in this position?
- What is the top priority for the person in this position over the next three months?
- What particular achievements would equate to success at this job?
- What are the qualities of successful managers in this company?

Interviewer - That person across from you, they are important and they count. You could be the only person who makes them feel that way today, do it.

- How long have you been with the company?
- Has your role changed since you've been here?
- What did you do before this?
- Why did you come to this company?
- What have you like most about working here?
- What do you like about working here?

The Company - Who do you work for? The company. You work for the company, not one boss, one department, but the company.

- I've read about the company's founding, but can you tell me more about the history?
- Where do you see this company in the next few years?
- What can you tell me about your new products or plans for growth?
- What are the current goals that the company is focused on, and how does this team work to support hitting those goals?
- What excites you most about the company's future?
- What do you think distinguishes this company from its competitors, both from a public and employee perspective?
- What is the company's management style?
- Is relocation to another company location a possibility?

The Team - Who will you work with? It can make all the difference in your happiness and job satisfaction.

- Can you tell me about the team I'll be working with?
- Who will I work with most closely?

- Who will I report to directly? Can I meet him or her?
- Who will report to me?
- What are their strengths and the team's biggest challenges?
- Do you expect to hire more people in this department in the next six months?
- Which other departments work most closely with this one?
- How many people work in this office/department?
- What kinds of processes are in place to help me work collaboratively?
- How can I best contribute to the department?

The Culture - What kind of environment is, what is the ecology? Conservative, wild, competitive, exciting, calm, cut-throat, cooperative? What kind of place are you stepping into, and is it what you will find a rewarding environment?

- What is the company and team culture like?
- How would you describe the work environment here, collaborative or more independent?
- Can you tell me about the last team event you did together?
- What's your favorite office tradition?
- What do you and the team usually do for lunch?
- Does anyone on the team get together outside the office?
- Do you ever do companywide events?
- What's different about working here than anywhere else you've worked?
- How has the company changed since you joined?
- How would you describe the company's culture and leadership philosophy?
- Can you give me some examples of the most desirable aspects of the company's culture?

Next Steps - Make sure you leave no questions about you in the interviewers mind and that you're clear on the next steps by asking questions.

- How do you see me as a candidate for the job in comparison with an ideal candidate?
- Now that we've talked about my qualifications and the job, do you have any concerns about my being successful in this position?
- Do you have any remaining questions about my qualifications?
- What are the next steps in the interview process?
- Is there anything else I can provide you with that would be helpful?
- Can I answer any final questions for you?
- Would you like a list of references?
- When do you think you will be making a decision?
- When can I expect to hear from you?
- If I am extended a job offer, how soon would you like me to start?
- This job sounds like something I'd really like to do, do you see a fit here, too?

It is possible that you might want to ask one of the following questions but don't. They are bad questions. You should have done a little research so you know the answer to some. The others are just questions that annoy or scare interviewers. Don't do it!

Interview Questions NOT to Ask (these are dumb questions)

- What does this company do?
- What's the company mission statement?

- If I get the job when can I take time off for vacation?
- Can I change my schedule if I get the job?
- Did I get the job?
- Do you do background checks?
- Do you monitor e-mail or Internet usage.

Interview Questions you will be asked

Here are a number of questions that you might ask in an interview. Keep in mind that you will not be asked all of these questions but you will be asked some of them, guaranteed.

These questions do not all fit or apply to every job. Highlight the ones that seem most appropriate to you and the job(s) you are seeking. Somewhere in your documentation, write down the questions you've highlighted, and then your answer to it. If you can answer all of the questions listed here, you are really prepared for an interview but it is not necessary to answer them all. Some of them are variations on the same theme.

Be sure to pay attention in interviews to questions that you haven't been asked before and put those in your documentation too, along with the best answer you can give when you have time to think about it. That's part of the experience and something to learn from. It's good to be prepared!

Plan on using the 30:60:90 rule to answer questions. Thirty seconds to answer most questions. Sixty seconds for some questions will make sense. Sixty seconds is a long time in an interview but there are times when a question will need a longer answer.

If you do prepare your answers to these questions, read your answers out loud. See how long it takes to read the longest answer out loud.

TV commercials seldom run more than sixty seconds. If they can sell a car, a credit card, a cell phone, a cell phone carrier, a breakfast, lunch or dinner, a house, an insurance company, whatever, in sixty seconds or less, then you should be able to answer a question in that time. If you are bumping into 90 seconds, you might need to work on answering that question before the next time you run into it.

One more tip: practice, practice, practice.

Common Basic Questions
Describe yourself or how would you describe yourself?
Are you overqualified for this job?
Are you the best person for this job? Why?
Are you willing to relocate?
Do you have any questions for me?
Is there anything else I can tell you about the job and the company?
Tell me why you want to work here.
What are you looking for in your next position?
What attracted you to this company?
What can you contribute to this company?
What can you do for this company?
What can you do for us that other candidates can't?

What do you know about our company or industry?
What interests you about this job?

What's your ideal company?
Why do you want this job?
Why should we hire you?

Work History
What relevant experience do you have?
What was the last project you headed up, and what was its outcome?
What were the responsibilities of your last position?
What did you like least about your last job?
What did you like or dislike about your previous job?
When were you most satisfied in your job?

Achievements & Accomplishments
Give me some examples of ideas you've had implemented.
Give me an example of a time that you felt you went above and beyond the call of duty at work.
Tell me about your proudest achievement.
What is your greatest achievement outside of work?
What major challenges have you handled?
What was your biggest accomplishment (failure) in your last position?

What are you like to work with (how do you fit in)?
Can you describe a time when your work was criticized?
Describe a difficult (experience, situation or project) at work and how you handled it.
Describe how you would handle a situation if you were required to finish multiple tasks by the end of the day, and there was no conceivable way that you could finish them.
Do you take work home with you?
Have you ever been on a team where someone was not pulling their own weight? How did you handle it?
Have you ever had difficulty working with a manager?
Have you gotten angry at work? What happened?
How do you feel about taking no for an answer?
How do you handle (stress, pressure)?
How would you feel about working for someone who knows less than you?
How would you feel about working for a (woman, foreigner, man, young person)?
If I were your supervisor and asked you to do something that you disagreed with, what would you do?
If you found out your company was doing something against the law, like fraud, what would you do?
If you were at a business lunch and you ordered a rare steak and they brought it to you well done, what would you do?
Tell me about a time when you had to give someone difficult feedback. How did you handle it?
Tell me about a time where you had to deal with conflict on the job.
What assignment was too difficult for you, and how did you resolve the issue?
What irritates you about other people, and how do you deal with it?
What is your greatest failure, and what did you learn from it?
What problems have you encountered at work?
What was the most difficult period in your life, and how did you deal with it?

What's the most difficult decision you've made in the last two years and how did you come to that decision?

How do you think I rate as an interviewer?

Goals

How do you want to improve yourself in the next year?

If I were to ask your last supervisor to provide you additional training or exposure, what would she suggest?

What are you looking for in terms of career development?

Describe your career goals.

What do you ultimately want to become?

How long do you expect to work for this company?

What are your goals for the future?

Where would you like to be in your career five years from now?

Culture & Values - Who are you?

Describe your best boss and your worst boss.

Give me an example of a time you did something wrong. How did you handle it?

How do you evaluate (measure) success?

If you were interviewing someone for this position, what traits would you look for?

What negative thing would your last boss say about you?

Do you think a leader should be feared or liked?

List five words that describe your character.

Tell me one thing about yourself you wouldn't want me to know.

Tell me the difference between good and exceptional.

Was there a person in your career who really made a difference?

What are the qualities of a (good or bad) leader?

What are three things your last boss would say about you?

What are you passionate about?

What challenges are you looking for in your next job?

What do you do in your spare time?

What do you expect from a supervisor?

What do you look for in terms of corporate culture?

What do you think of your previous boss?

What is your personal mission statement?

What kind of personality do you work best with and why?

What three character traits would your friends use to describe you?

What was most (least) rewarding about your job?

What will you do if you don't get a job offer?

What will you miss about your present/last job?

What's the most important thing you learned in school?

What is your greatest fear?

What is your biggest regret and why?

Why did you choose your major?

If the people who know you were asked why you should be hired, what would they say?

Performance & Evaluation - what can we expect from you?

How long will it take for you to make a significant contribution?

How would you go about establishing your credibility quickly with the team?

If selected for this position, can you describe your strategy for the first 90 days?
What do you see yourself doing within the first 30 days of this job?

Salary

How much do you expect to get paid?
What are your salary requirements?
What were your starting and final levels of compensation?
What's your salary history?

Work Context

Do you prefer to work alone or on a team?
Give some examples of your work as a team member or leader.
Is there a type of work environment you prefer?
What techniques and tools do you use to keep yourself organized?
What would be your ideal working environment?
Describe your use and competence with computer technology.

Work Styles

Describe your work style.
How would you describe the pace at which you work?
If you had to choose one, would you consider yourself a big-picture person or a detail-oriented person?

My Marketing Plan

In the book, "It's Your Future" we discuss all of the elements in a thorough personal marketing plan. You should be able to fill-in all of the blanks in the following material. If you cannot, that indicates that you have over-looked something and you may want to spend some time on it.

Unique Selling Proposition (25 words or less): _____

_____

_____

_____

_____

_____

On the next few pages is a layout for analyzing a job target and comparing yourself to it. This helps you see yourself in the job, which you will use in further steps of your marketing. You should consider making copies of this section and filling one out for each job target you have.

Be sure to look at jobs that match your job zones levels. If you aren't sure what that means, you can review it in the book, "It's Your Future" or go the Dept. of Labor's O*NET website (onetonline.org).

Phase 1: Preparation

Goals (Identify Personally Rewarding factors and your job and career goals): _____

_____

_____

_____

_____

_____

Job Target: _____

What Knowledge is required? _____

_____

_____

_____

_____

List your knowledge and where you acquired it? _____

_____

_____

_____

_____

What Skills are required? _____

_____

_____

_____

_____

List your skills: _____

_____

_____

_____

_____

What Abilities are required? _____

_____

_____

_____

_____

List your abilities: _____

_____

_____
_____
_____
_____

What Personality factors are involved? _____
_____
_____
_____
_____
_____

Describe (list) your personality factors? _____
_____
_____
_____
_____
_____

What Tools and Technology is involved? _____
_____
_____
_____
_____

What Tools and Technology can you use? _____
_____
_____
_____

What are the Educational requirements? _____
_____
_____
_____

What is your Education (Include all training programs, 1 day to 2+years in length, and mention any special awards earned)? _____
_____
_____
_____

Phase 1: Preparation (continued)

Where do you want to live? _____
_____
_____

Are you willing to re-locate? Yes No Maybe

How far from home are you willing to travel on the job? _____

How far from home are you willing to travel to and from the job? _____

What kind of company do you want to work for?

Your preferences (in order of priority):

First: _____
Second: _____
Third: _____

What combined package of wage and benefits are you seeking? Here you should consider everything you want from a job and if it doesn't include it, increase the wage you are seeking because you will have to pay for it if the employer doesn't. Some jobs include all of these benefits and more! Circle each item that you consider important to you in this section and then estimate your target "Wage". Ask for 20% more than that if asked.

Insurance:
  Medical - Yes No
  Dental - Yes No
  Optical - Yes No
  Life - Yes No
  Accidental Death - Yes No
  Disability - Yes No
Extra Pay
  Raises - Yes No
  Bonuses - Yes No
  Overtime - Yes No
Leave
  Vacation - Yes No
  Paid Holidays - Yes No
  Sick/personal - Yes No

Retirement
  Pension Plans - Yes No
  401(k) Plans - Yes No
  Profit sharing - Yes No
  Stock options/ESOPs - Yes No
Other benefits
  Tuition Reimbursement - Yes No
  Dependent Care - Yes No
  Employee Assistance Programs
  - Yes No
  Parking - Yes No
  Expense Reimbursements
      - Yes No
  Travel Expenses - Yes No
  Expense Accounts - Yes No

Wage: _____

Pre-search Preparation:

Resumes Prepared (and error free):
Generic: Yes No
Chronological: Yes No

Functional: Yes No

References (Name, address, phone, relationship to you):

1: _____
   _____

2: _____
   _____

3: _____
   _____

4: _____
   _____

5: _____
   _____

Cover letter: Do you have one you are comfortable with to use as a model? Yes/No

Phone Preparation: Phone response record pad? Yes No

Online Preparation:

Social media presence reviewed? Yes No
Acceptable? Yes No
Email address for job hunt? Yes No
(Don't forget to check your spam folder for responses)

Tracking System:
A calendar system (or documenting system) that works for you, ready? Yes/No

Documentation prepared?
   Letters of Reference: Yes No
   Training Certificates: Yes No
   Diploma's: Yes No
   Driver's License: Yes No
   Proof of Insurance: Yes No
   Trade Certification: Yes No
If you are going to be asked to "prove it", do you have proof? Some applications will require you to arrange to have it sent directly, like college diploma's. Do you have the address to contact to make those arrangements? If not, get it. Prepare, remember?

Interviews: Practiced, comfortable? Yes No

Job leads and contacts - do you know where they are?:
   List of potential employers of interest? Yes No
   Job Postings/Recruitment Advertising? Yes No

Job Fairs? Yes No
Making Cold Calls? Yes No
Using Your Network? Yes No
Job-hunting on the Web? Yes No
University Career Centers Job Postings(they aren't limited to students as a rule)
 Yes No
Alumni Offices of schools (you went too)? Yes No
Headhunters & Recruiters at Executive Search Firms? Yes No
Public & Private /Employment Agencies? Yes No

Phase 2: Activation (Implementation) Action

Nothing is accomplished without action being taken. Nothing. You have to activate your plan. Use it to guide your actions. Review this list frequently!

1. Apply for jobs.
    a. Vary your approach
    b. Start with your target list
    c. Do it!
    d. Keep track of where and when you applied.
    e. On applications, follow the directions completely.
    f. Organize your job hunting for efficiency.
    g. Try to engage the hiring manager.
    h. How did you get each interview?
    i. How did you handle any telephone interviews?
    j. Did you rehearse telephone interviews?
    k. Did you being your "cheat sheet" with you to make filling out an application easier?

2. Interviews.
    a. Dressed "right"
    b. Brought supporting materials (resumes, references, copies of transcripts, certifications, etc.)?
    c. Used Interview Checklist?
    d. Prepared, practiced, have USP, STARs, and ready for tough, embarrassing questions.
    e. Relaxed yet eager for the opportunity?

3. Post Interview:
    a. Sent a hand-signed thank you letter or note.
    b. Followed up as you committed?
    c. Called back and re-pitched.
    d. If offered job, prepared to negotiate?
    e. If job obtained, informed and thanked everyone who helped.

Remember to Evaluate Daily, Weekly and Monthly.

Strengths, Weaknesses, Opportunities, Threats (SWOT) Analysis:

As a person and as an employee:

My strengths: _____
_____
_____
_____

My weaknesses are: _____
_____
_____
_____

My opportunities are: _____
_____
_____
_____

My threats are: _____
_____
_____
_____

If you have a handle on your SWOT, you can sell your strengths and be aware of your weaknesses (not necessarily work on them, just be aware of them). You can seek your opportunities and use "threats" as motivators to find your Most Rewarding Job and Career future.

Stress

As an exercise, circle the things on the following lists that have popped up in your life. There are some blank spaces for you to add your own stress-inducing events and situations. Be aware of the fact that not all stressors are negative, getting married, having a baby or adopting one, buying a house or a new car, are some examples of positive but stressful events.

Stressful Events:

- Death of a spouse
- Divorce
- Marital separation
- Death of a close family member
- Personal injury or illness
- Wedding
- Dismissal from work
- Marital reconciliation
- Retirement
- Change in health of family member
- Pregnancy
- Sexual difficulties
- Gain a new family member
- Business readjustment
- Sudden change in financial state
- Obtaining major mortgage
- Foreclosure of mortgage or loan
- Child leaving home
- Outstanding personal achievement
- Spouse starts or stops work
- Begin or end of school year
- Revision of personal habits
- Obtaining minor loan
- Buying a car
- Taking a Vacation
- Christmas, shopping and holidays
- Minor violation of law
- Flat tire on car
- House destroyed in a calamity
- Floods
- Fires
- Death of a pet
- _____
- _____
- _____
- _____

Chronic, long term situations and conditions:

- Marital problems

- Problems with children
- Problems with parents
- Problems with co-workers
- Problems with business partners
- Long term business problems
- Change in sleeping habits
- Imprisonment
- Personal Injury or Illness
- Adjusting to marriage
- Retirement
- Pregnancy
- Business readjustments
- Change in responsibilities at work
- Problems with in-laws
- Change in living conditions
- Revision of personal habits
- Problems with a boss
- Change in working hours or conditions
- Change in residence
- Change in schools
- Change in recreation
- Change in church activities
- Change in social activities
- Change in eating habits
- Mental health issues
- Recurrent car trouble
- Transportation problems
- Job dissatisfaction
- Too much to do
- Money problems
- Drug and alcohol abuse
- Gambling addiction
- Other addictions, like to video games and cellphones
- Relationship problems with friends
- Relationship problems with significant others
- _____
- _____
- _____
- _____
- _____
- _____
- _____
- _____

Self Awareness - it starts with you recognizing that you are feeling excess stress or distressed. How do you know when you are feeling stressed? Think about it and write it down (document it). What are your signs?

Identify the Problems - if you're feeling distressed it is almost always more than one thing that is impacting you in a short span of time, even while other things are causing you long term chronic stress. Take a few minutes and write down as many of those things as you can (use the list for some ideas but don't stop there, there are probably others). Don't forget to write down things that you've had to put aside, or give up for awhile, the things that give you pleasure. Not having them in your life, even for a short while, is a problem because not having a pleasure, a reward, a "rest and relaxation" thing in your life is a stressor too! Can you put any of those things back in your life?

Break each problem down into its parts.

Solve the problems you can solve:
- Are there parts that you can do somethings about?
    - Parts you can delay?
    - Parts that are so far in the future you can forget about them for now?
- Sometimes you need to cope with stress by having an adult conversation with others. It isn't easy. give it try though.
- Live with some problems, by themselves they aren't a big deal.
- Live with other problems, they are big deals but not within your control to do anything about them. Usually these are "facts of life" like you bought a house, or a family member passed away. Acceptance of some events as unhappy, or happy, life events is something we do. Consider short term counseling, grief counseling, or talking with your doctor.
- Let it go. Tough advice but if things in the past are nagging at you, haunting you, bugging you still, and you find yourself carrying, nursing, and holding a grudge, try to forgive, to let it go, accept that sometimes that's life. Move on. Set it down, as the stinky, dirty baggage it is. It's not your fault it happened, why should you hang on to it? Let it go and walk away from it. Remember success may be the best revenge you can get.
- Avoid the unacceptable, intolerable and downright repugnant. Get away from obnoxious people, change lanes, slow down or speed up and get away from bad drivers, stop listening to complainers, walk away.
- Make changes - in yourself, your relationships, your lifestyle. Change your thoughts and actions. Hint: It's easier to change yourself than the other person and that is tough enough, isn't it? Still ...

Reflect on what you've done, the problem solving action steps you took and the results you've achieved. Doing something is the best tonic. Is your stress back to normal? If not, repeat and keep working on it. It's not that you failed, you're not just done yet.

Other ideas to reduce stress or cope with it:

- Get a new job.
- Get new friends.
- Drop problem-inducing people form your life, if you can.
- Lower your expectations, take the pressure off yourself.
- Maintain emotionally supportive relationships or get some.
- Learn and practice calming techniques.
- Take up yoga.
- Listen to plain chants (Gregorian Chants).
- Learn and practice relaxation training.

- Change your lifestyle.
- Exercise daily.
- Improve your eating habits.
- Drop bad habits.
- Be honest with yourself.
- Take a long walk outdoors.
- Catch Your Breath - step out of what's happening for a few minutes.
- Practice "calming, breathing techniques".
- Play a team sport.
- Get a massage.
- Give a massage.
- Do something about your physical health:
  - See a doctor
  - Talk to someone about your problems
  - Get Advice and Follow It
  - Work on it
  - Eat Right
  - Get Enough Sleep
  - Exercise
  - Relax
- Not enough money? Trim your budget.
  - Drop cable tv.
  - Eliminate or reduce phone costs.
  - Cut out extras.
  - Use the library instead of buying books, music, etc.

Be proactive and work on reducing and eliminating excess stress. Treat stress management as a an exercise in problem solving and don't let them pile up.

Replace these words in your life:

depressed	jealous	weak	dissatisfied
worn out	angry	inferior	broken
withdrawn	useless	whipped	frustrated
blue	bored	beaten	tired of it all
hopeless	worthless	suicidal	incompetent
neglected	powerless	gypped	down
ignored	have regrets	cheated	anxious
lost	worried	denied	drained
lonely	fearful	uncompetitive	antsy
envious	scared	less than	

Try to eliminate the negative in your life. Highlight or circle all the things you have been feeling lately. Then make a conscious decision, choose not to continue feeling that way. Get help if you need it. Talk it out with someone. Read a book about it and how to overcome it. Google, Bing or whatever your choice of search engine is and ask it "how to not be _____" or "how to deal with _____" or "coping with _____". Do not let your life continue to be dominated by negativity. It doesn't have to be like that.

So replace those negative words in your life with these words:

excited	free	accepting	dynamic
happy	encouraged	thankful	tenacious
alive	sympathetic	great	challenged
good	marvelous	reassured	open
optimistic	wonderful	positive	hopeful
confident	resilient	loving	calm
reliable	upbeat	eager	cheerful
energetic	kind	unique	content
at ease	considerate	curious	enthusiastic
fortunate	refreshed	determined	

What can you do today to put one of these words in your life? Can you be kind or considerate to someone, including yourself? How about tomorrow, could you choose to be feel great and alive tomorrow? Sure you can. You've made it this far, think how far you can still go.

96166659R00078

Made in the USA
San Bernardino, CA
18 November 2018